# The Shepherdess

## A Story of Faith and Family

### By

### Rick Birk

Copyright 2010 by Rick Birk

ISBN no. 978-0-9819964-3-1

Library of Congress categories: Religious ethics. Individual ethics. Character. Virtue. Women in comparative religion. Religious education. Creeds, confessions, covenants. Christian symbols and symbolism. Prayer. Moral education. Moral theology. Practical religion. The Christian life. Genealogy.

This book is easily available at go5books.com

# What people are saying about *The Shepherdess*

"Long before the Second Vatican Council reminded all of us about the 'universal call to holiness,' simple yet sincere people like Dorothy were already answering that call. Jesus had a description for Dorothy—'salt of the earth, light to the world.'"

-*Most Reverend Timothy M. Dolan - Archbishop of New York*

"*The Shepherdess* is a son-in-law's unique tribute to his mother-in-law and her love for all who were a part of her life. Take a seat at the Wiencek dining room table – Dorothy already set a place for you – and feast on a smorgasbord of wisdom and grace that binds children and their spouses, grandchildren and friends in the fabric of faith. You'll feel like a part of the family, which is what Dorothy would expect."

-*Brian Olszewski, Executive Editor/G.M.*
*The Catholic Herald, Milwaukee, Wisconsin*

"*The Shepherdess* is a lovely book. It is a true testimony to a person's faith and living life by God's standards."

-*Larcy Dunford, MC LPC Therapist*
*Christian Counseling Center of Scottsdale*

"What a beautiful book about a true Shepherdess, and a real living Saint–DOROTHY. It takes us deep into her faith and spirituality."

- *Deacon Mike Cesarec, Milwaukee, Wisconsin*

"We are taught that saints weren't born that way, but were real people. The inverse is also true, that real people become saints. Rick Birk's story of his mother-in-law Dorothy and her family is filled with tales of overcoming adversity and service to others through abiding faith, as well as a collection of beautiful prayers and humorous anecdotes. It's an inspiration for any family seeking to live as God intended us to live."

-*Mark J. Scarp, Journalist -Journalism Instructor, Scottsdale, Arizona*

# Acknowledgements

John Birk
Tom Birk
Brad Cooper (Cooper design Studios)

# Dedication

This book is dedicated to Dorothy and Ervin Wiencek. I thank you from the bottom of my heart for so graciously welcoming me into your family. Your strength, resolve, and courage–examples of your uncompromising faith–have truly inspired your flock.

Love,
Rick

## Prologue

# ERVIN

### The Jabez Prayer

And Jabez called on the God of Israel saying,

"Oh, that You would bless me indeed,

and enlarge my territory,

that Your hand would be with me,

and that You would keep me from evil,

That I may not cause pain!"

So God granted him what he requested.

−1 Chronicles 4:10

Life gives us the opportunity to make significant progress on our divine path. Along the way, beacons of light in the form of spiritual change agents greet us at every turn in the road. They appear in many forms and associations. If we are cognizant, we can recognize them and heed their messages. Dorothy Christine Wiencek, the matriarch of the Wiencek family, has not only embraced herself in this role, but elevated herself to include a responsibility likened to that of a shepherdess guiding her sheep on their true and everlasting path to righteousness. Due to her constant nurturing, devout leadership, and unshakeable faith in the Lord, her flock has enlarged and matured through the years.

I am very fortunate to have been an inspired member since 1973. Her flock has expanded well beyond family members to include neighbors, friends, and even total strangers. Dorothy is truly in the presence of the Lord in all of her thoughts, deeds, and actions. Her prayers and random acts of kindness have reached numerous recipients through the years. She truly is one with the Lord. An old Chinese Proverb states, "When someone shares something of value with you and you benefit from it, you have a moral obligation to share it with others." Herein lies my motivation for telling this story.

"Believe me when I say that I am in the Father and the Father is in me; or at least believe on the evidence of the miracles themselves. I tell you the truth, anyone who has faith in me will do what I have been doing. He will do even greater things than these, because I am going to the Father."
–John 14:11-12

# Christine Dorothy

*Christine, the first of Dorothy's eleven children, was born October 5, 1952. Her name was derived from Dorothy's middle name. Christine served as the maid of honor in my wedding. I still remember driving her and my future wife Terry to the UW-Milwaukee for classes. We shared many great moments and laughs. To this day, we still share a common bond–a love of ice cream.*

## Prayer to St. Christina

St. Christina, you lived a life of poverty and loneliness in the eyes of others. But you knew that in the eyes of God, you were wealthy and had His love and the companionship of saints and angels. Help us to see beyond the things of the world and to realize we are never alone with God and that we are surrounded by a "great cloud of witnesses that have gone before us." Pray that we remember to offer up our sufferings for those who do not see beyond the material and who are seeking love and fulfillment, that they may come to know God and realize that they are never alone. Amen.

My first recollection of religion can be traced back to Christmas, 1956 at the ripe old age of five. I distinctly remember the uproar my brother Tom caused when we attended Christmas Eve service at St. John Lutheran Church in Milwaukee. At age nine, he was utterly amazed at the sheer size and brilliance of the beautifully lit Christmas tree on display at the front of the church just off the side of the lectern. As the overflow

## The Shepherdess

crowd hurried in to find seats, he ran up to the tree to get a better look. For a brief second, he reached out to touch and validate the majestic overpowering sign of Christmas. His hand grasped a tree branch. A little tug ensued. The twenty-five-foot tree rocked back and forth briefly as the shocked congregation looked on. Then, the worst fears were realized. To the shrieks and groans of the congregation, the tree came tumbling down. My parents were shocked and embarrassed. As they ushered Tom away from the toppled tree, they sheepishly offered their apologies. The rest of the service is a blur, but my introduction to the Lord's birthday is one I will never forget.

Merry Christmas, Baby Jesus!

In the summer of 1957 we moved to Delafield, Wisconsin. My parents loved this small town. Years earlier, they had met at a picnic in Delafield's Cushing Park. For the record, our family's move was prompted by my dad's job transfer to Watertown, not by popular demand of the St. John's congregation!

We settled uneventfully into quaint, neighborly Delafield. In many ways the small town mirrored the simplicity of so many others. Often I've thought of it as Wisconsin's "Mayberry." At the time, downtown Delafield actually had several two-story buildings and, like most towns in Wisconsin, no shortage of local 'watering holes' like Zunker's Tap and Robert E. Lee's.

Our lazy community, snug on the shore of Lake Nagawicka, came complete with its cast of rural characters.

Rollie the barber cut everyone's hair in the local "Rollie's." Mr. Shuman owned the town bakery, a definite family favorite, aptly named "Shuman's Bakery." The police chief, the dad of one of my classmates, held his post only in a part-time capacity. The lack of criminal activity did not warrant a full-time position.

My mother, once a devout Catholic, had converted to Lutheran when she married Dad. Our family continued in the faith and attended Delafield Lutheran Church (Missouri Synod). Pastor Ralph Huget welcomed us into this quaint church on the west side of town. The church was much smaller than our previous church in Milwaukee. In the back of their minds, Mom and Dad must have thought that a shorter, sturdier Christmas tree would be the logical choice of this congregation!

On my mother's side, the family had been Catholic for the last several generations. However, other beliefs had been interwoven into our heritage. One ancestor, Joseph Church, had been a pioneer minister who traveled the Oregon Trail in the 1840s, preaching the word of the Lord, before he settled in Long Beach County, Washington. In a series of now-published letters ("The Church Letters") to his daughter and son-in-law, he expressed his strong Christian beliefs. It took courage and strong faith to forge through the wilderness, in such unsettling times. Each day he faced uncertainty about if and when he would see his family again. On June 23, 1883, he wrote from Oysterville, Washington:

## The Shepherdess

*We would like to know if you are trying to live a Christian life. That is what we want more than anything is to be Christians. To know that our sins are forgiven, that we are accepted of God and have his spirit dwelling in us continuously and feel to rejoice in the hope of glory. May God help you both to give yourselves up to God and serve him the rest of your days so if we never meet again on earth, we can meet in heaven where there will be no more sorrow, no more parting, where we can gather around the Throne of God and sing praises unto him forever and ever.*

Joseph Church believed in the joy and rewards of everlasting life. He was passionate about sharing the message of God's love for, and forgiveness of, his children. It is a message that has been passed through the generations.

Prior to our move to Delafield, my oldest brother John had started his coursework for confirmation at our former church in Milwaukee, and was confirmed at St. John's Lutheran Church in 1956. However, as years went by I noticed that John attended church only on holidays and that my dad came seldom if ever. However, my brother Tom, unfazed by the ghost of Christmas past, became a model Christian. He, Mom and I attended every week. Tom and I also attended Bible school each summer for many years. Tom went on to be confirmed in the faith and joined Luther League, a weekly youth ministry. He even entertained thoughts of becoming a minister.

By the time Tom had started high school, John had received and accepted an appointment to West Point. Both John and Tom had attended St. John's Military Academy, a college-prep high school offering a top-notch education. When it came my turn, however, my brothers urged me to enroll at a new local high school with my friends. I took their advice and attended Kettle Moraine High School.

With Pastor Huget's retirement on the horizon, a new minister, Pastor Paul Christiansen, joined our congregation. He brought to our church a more youthful, spirited, energetic look. I remember as a child praying only when I needed God's help. But Pastor Christiansen encouraged us to pray daily, to express our gratitude regularly for all the gifts God provides in our lives.

This reminds me of a homily I once heard. A young boy prayed to the Lord for a shiny, brand-new, red bike. Amid his prayer, he scrawled his request on a piece of paper–"Lord, if you give me this new bike, I will be good to my little brother for four whole weeks." He thought for a second, then crumbled up the paper and threw it in the wastebasket. He started again, "Lord, if you give me this new bike, I'll be good to my little brother for three weeks." Again having second thoughts, he crumbled the paper and threw it away. After a few more moments of reflection, he jumped up from his desk, grabbed a stool, and climbed up and retrieved a shoebox from the top shelf of his closet. He walked over to his dresser, carefully picked up a statue

## The Shepherdess

of the Blessed Mother, placed the statue into the box, and returned the box to the top shelf, behind some of his clothes. Again he sat down at his desk, and started again. "Dear Jesus," he wrote. "If you ever want to see your Mother again...."

The point here? We should pray with gratitude, not attitude! Since prayer is such a powerful force, our prayers should express what we *truly* want, not what we *think* we want. Prayer itself can help us distinguish the difference. I've come to realize that we should be careful what we pray for, because God may well grant us our request.

Consider the following story:

A spacious new church had been recently completed beside a vacant lot. A man purchased the adjoining parcel lot and intended to build, of all things, a tavern. Hearing the news, the congregation grew very upset and started to pray fervently for the man to have a change of heart. Never the less, the bar was built. Members of the church began to pray that a fire would destroy the bar. Within three weeks, a bolt of lightning struck and destroyed the tavern, burning it to the ground. The upset bartender sued the church. After all, didn't the prayers of the congregation cause the destruction? In court, a representative defended the church, saying, "Just because we prayed, it doesn't mean that it would come true." At the conclusion of the hearing, the wise, elderly judge momentarily scratched his chin, peered up from his papers, and announced, "Ladies and gentlemen, this *is* a very interesting case. On the one hand, you have a bartender who believes in the power of prayer–and on the other, a church that doesn't!"

It was soon my turn to start Confirmation classes. I would be the second Birk confirmed at Delafield Lutheran Church. I remember being very uninterested in the coursework and found any (and every) excuse to avoid class. The classes were not very conveniently scheduled and often conflicted with my sports and other activities. In hindsight, I see how my priorities of athletics and social events were immature and misplaced, although at the time they seemed appropriate. I managed to struggle through and succeeded, by the skin of my teeth. I will never forget Pastor Paul's advice to us moments before our all-important "questioning" (a query of religious knowledge in front of the congregation). He confided to us, if we were unsure of the correct answer to a question, to reply, "The Lord Jesus!" We were assured that this response would be appropriate for many of the questions.

It worked! I was confirmed a Lutheran.

Our congregation continued to grow. Before long, our small, cozy church could no longer accommodate all of its members. The logical next step was to move to a new, larger site. With the financial support of the Pastor and congregation, construction of a new church began. For a year or so my attendance dwindled to major holidays and special occasions. Then suddenly, God sent me an inspiration. Her name was Diane. I started dating her shortly after her family moved to Delafield and became members

## The Shepherdess

of our church. Motivation comes in all shapes and sizes. Mine was blonde and 5' 7". Yes, God works in mysterious ways. Once again I was attending regularly. About a year later, our lovely, new church was complete, and Delafield Lutheran Church was reborn. To match its splendor, it was renamed Christ the King Lutheran Church.

The summer before my senior year of high school, I had the opportunity to work for a neighbor and fellow-parishioner, William Timm. He had built many of the fireplaces that still warm many homes in Delafield and surrounding communities. A mason by trade, Bill needed help and hired me as a mason's tender for the summer. The work was tedious, and the days were long. But I made good money. More importantly, I took from Bill a lifetime of benefits–a foundation for the future. Bill was a hard worker, a man of ethics and integrity. Also, he taught me the jargon of masonry. A hammer was called a "persuader." Cement was "mud." Tool compartments on the sides of the truck were "pigeonholes." I learned to drive a stick shift by taking the 1956 truck on a cement run. Very simply, Bill Timm's successful business was based on trust. His most important asset was–his word.

Until I left for college, I attended Sunday services with Mom and Diane several times a month. I enjoyed these special times with my mother and Diane, which often led to deeply involved spiritual discussions. My mom impressed upon me the need for an unwavering faith and belief in the Lord. "God's ways are not our ways. He always has a Master Plan," she would often tell me. With her strong faith, she emphasized, "A world without God makes no sense. God is a central part of our belief system, the very foundation of our morals and ethics."

After high school, I went off to college. Like many young people, I found myself faced with a host of new responsibilities and as a result many changes. With geographic distance between us, Diane and I drifted apart. Even though things didn't work out for us, I was extremely fortunate to have had such a wonderful Christian as my girlfriend. She influenced me in many ways that I will never forget.

Growth and change continued to challenge me. If the break-up wasn't enough, a variety of circumstances found my once cohesive family scattered in many directions; each pursuing an individual path. A week after Tom graduated from Carroll College, he received the dreaded letter from the local draft board. Before we knew it, he was an enlisted member of the U.S. Navy training in Pensacola, Florida, and was soon transferred to Germany. John attended graduate school at the UW-Milwaukee. Finally, my parents had sold our house in Delafield and moved to Oregon, to be in closer proximity to my mom's mother. I remained behind at the UW-Milwaukee on a basketball scholarship.

In the summer of 1970, John and I drove to Tucson, Arizona, for a wedding. After, we headed east to Pensacola, Florida to see Tom, at Naval Intelligence School. We bought some food and decided to picnic on the white-

## The Shepherdess

sand beach. As we ate, we spotted a girl farther down the beach, testing the waves. After eating, I decided to hike along the beach. As I neared her I heard, "Hi, Rick!" We both started laughing, and walked back together to meet my brothers. This "Florida beauty" was from Nashota, Wisconsin—just two miles north of Delafield. I knew her from my confirmation classes. At that moment, I realized it was indeed a small, small world!

Over the next few years I dated a few girls but could not make the spiritual connection I felt was needed for a relationship to blossom. I was at a crossroads, searching for answers to questions such as, "Who am I? What is my purpose? What should I do as a career?" I missed seeing my family every day, missed all the laughs and good times we had shared through the years. Up until that time, we had been blessed to have each other close by. Memories of wonderful times shared with my family, made the emptiness even more painful.

Sports had always been important to my family. Many great family memories centered on athletic events. My brothers and I played multiple sports. We were each other's biggest fans. It was such a void to no longer be able to enjoy these often-daily games and activities. So much change in such a short period had taken its toll. I felt lost. I didn't know what to do next, which direction to head. It is often said that, when one door closes, another opens. However, being nineteen, I usually pried doors open for myself, at my own furious pace. It was much like shaking a muddy glass of water in an effort to make it clear. The answer of course, is found with time and settling, not shaking the glass. Amid our problems and challenges in life, patience and maturity teach us that shaking the glass keeps the residue from settling. Left alone, the sediment will eventually sink. It is similar to how God works, in His own timeframe. Experience has shown me that faith and trust in the Lord is all you need.

In the late fall of 1971, a friend and I were 'hanging out' in the UWM student union when he noticed two girls seated at a nearby table. We walked over and introduced ourselves. My friend flashed a deck of cards he had along and, with a wink, challenged them to a game of cards. Surprisingly, they accepted. We agreed on a wager. The losers would have to clean the winners' dorm rooms. As we explained the game, our confidence soared. It quickly grew apparent that they had never played the game and did not grasp how to play it well. In less than an hour, we had won. I wasted no time scheduling my "new maid Terry" to clean my room. A good sport, she agreed to come at 2:00 p.m., after her sociology class.

Promptly at 2:00 pm, I heard a soft knock. I opened the door to see Terry, true to her word, standing outside. With her long brunette hair, she was a real beauty. Although I have always been extremely neat, on this occasion I had intentionally left my room in disarray–had even scattered clothes around the room just before her arrival. She quickly got to work. As she straightened up the room we

## The Shepherdess

chatted, and I came to learn more about her. She was a nursing student, extremely bright. Only seventeen, she had graduated valedictorian at St. Joan Antida, a private, all-girls high school only a few months before. She was very efficient. In less than an hour my entire room was once again neat and tidy. The scent of pine cleaner hung heavily, and added to the fresh, clean appearance. The job done, she announced that she had a lot of homework, and left.

Over the next few weeks, we occasionally bumped into each other, mostly in the student union where we had met. One cold day, I offered to drive her home from school, so that she did not have to take the city bus, her usual means of transportation.

Nothing could have prepared me for what I was about to encounter.

# Therese Marie

*Terry, the second-oldest daughter, was born on October 11, 1953. She was named after St. Therese, a beloved saint of her mother Dorothy. Now married for thirty-six years, Terry and I have two wonderful children, Nicole and Jonathan. With her Masters degree in nursing and innate ability to nurture and aid, Terry is wonderfully prepared to help others. Her inner beauty is her finest quality.*

## Prayer to Saint Therese

O little St. Therese of the Child Jesus, who during your short life on earth became a mirror of angelic purity, of love strong as death, and of wholehearted abandonment to God, now that you rejoice in the reward of your virtues, cast a glance of pity on me as I leave all things in your hands. Make my troubles your own–speak a word for me to our Lady Immaculate, whose flower of special love you were– to that Queen of heaven 'who smiled on you at the dawn of life.' Beg her as the Queen of the heart of Jesus to obtain for me by her powerful intercession, the grace I yearn for so ardently at this moment, and that she join with it a blessing that may strengthen me during life. Defend me at the hour of death, and lead me straight on to a happy eternity. Amen.

Although cold and crisp, it was a bright, sunny, fall afternoon as Terry and I pulled up to her home on Milwaukee's north side. On the corner of 38th Street and Rochelle Avenue stood a two-story white house with green shutters surrounded by freshly cut

## The Shepherdess

grass and neatly trimmed shrubs. As I entered, an overwhelming sense of peace enveloped me. The home itself was immaculate. Religious pictures and statues occupied the living room, but a prominent picture on the center of the living room wall commanded my attention. It was apparent that this picture held significant importance. I soon learned it was an image of Our Mother of Perpetual Help.

Terry's mother Dorothy and Terry's youngest sister, four-year old Becky, greeted us. The rest of the family was at work or school. Dorothy, appearing to be in her early forties, was a small, physically fit woman with dark hair and an engaging smile. With her braided hair, little Becky was as cute as a button. After introductions, we sat around the kitchen table and talked for more than an hour. Every few minutes, Dorothy offered food and drinks. I was far too shy to accept.

I learned that Terry was the second-oldest of eleven children–she had *ten* brothers and sisters! What's more, the house had only four bedrooms. I was shocked. "Where does everyone sleep?" I asked, and was informed that Erv and Dorothy had one bedroom. The two boys, Frank and Paul, shared the second of the bedrooms downstairs. That meant—incredibly—nine girls all lived upstairs in two bedrooms and shared a single bathroom! All I could think of was sardines lined up in a very small can. Dorothy explained how smoothly things ran, and how blessed they were to be in their new home. I was in awe. With schedules and a message board, Dorothy worked all day long cooking, cleaning, washing, and grocery shopping. This left her with a few precious hours to sleep. Busy 24-7, she was extremely happy. I seriously thought that she *must* have a background as an air traffic controller at LaGuardia. Despite her ever-busy schedule, she took ample time to get to know me and made me feel uniquely welcome in their home.

As we continued to talk, I found Dorothy to be completely honest and forthright. I had never met a more personable, caring person. She was wholly accommodating, with a wonderful sense of humor. She made references to the Lord as if it were normal conversation to do so. For her it certainly was. Truly, the Lord always *has* been a big part of her life. She referred to Him as if speaking of another member of her family. Finally, I noticed that whenever Dorothy got up to do anything, it was always at an accelerated pace, with utter purpose.

I left that day in awe and amazement. Dorothy had honestly impressed me. She reminded me of a combination of Edith Bunker and Mother Teresa, two individuals who have willingly given up their lives for others!

Terry and I had a date for the following Friday night. I really looked forward to it. I couldn't wait to see Dorothy and Becky again and hoped to meet the others. I now had a better understanding of how Terry had developed her sense of compassion. As I drove over to pick up Terry, I found myself wondering, "Was Dorothy for real? She was so different, so … one of a kind. Had I just met her on a good day? Had she maybe tried to impress me?"

## The Shepherdess

Within moments of arrival, I realized I couldn't have been more wrong. That night Pat, a younger sister, greeted me and ushered me into the house and into the living room. Dorothy, as cordial as ever, stepped in quickly to welcome me. One by one I met the whole family–a very cumbersome process, to say the least. Terry's dad, home from work, was very pleasant, although he didn't say much.

The kids were all very friendly, and neatly dressed. After the introductions were completed, Pat quipped, "O.K. Rick–you need to repeat everyone's name before you can leave." It took me over a month to accomplish that feat! Finally on our way out the door, Pat ever the joker, with a smirk on her face and twinkle in her eye, had one final question for me, "Do you have honorable intentions for my sister?" she asked. The question drew hearty laughs from everyone. Once in the car, I told Terry that I was really impressed with everyone–even Pat. I had never had a personal encounter with such a large, and apparently happy family.

After that date, Terry and I were officially "going together." We saw each other almost every day. I was now a regular guest at her home, at least twice a week. The Wienceks were a very generous family. Dorothy would always insist that I stay to eat. Whenever I stepped in, an extra plate was set. I didn't want to say no and offend her, but with her large family and so many to feed, I was embarrassed to eat. Yet remarkably, Dorothy always seemed to have enough food for all. Typically on the menu were casseroles and stews with lots of vegetables. To cut costs, powered milk was added to regular and sometimes a little water to the orange juice, in order to make them stretch. It really reminded me of the parable of Jesus feeding the multitudes with the fish and the loaves. Yes, Mom always said there was plenty for everyone, and indeed there was. She understood that sharing food as Jesus did would do more than just feed us. It would break down people barriers. How gracious the Wiencek family was! Mom confided to me that once, years before, she had called social services because of the hardship of feeding all the children. The agency had told her that Erv's income was right on the borderline. As such, they were ineligible for assistance. Then Mom turned to me and emphasized, "I was proud and happy that we made it on our own." Mom did however, accept hand-me-down clothes, from relatives and neighbors, which certainly helped.

 Several weeks later I found myself in a deep conversation with Dorothy. I asked about her past, her life growing up, and how she met her husband, Erv. She was more than willing to share her stories. I learned that the Wiencek family was 100% Polish. Erv's parents were both of Polish descent. Likewise, Dorothy's mother, Katherine Habrat and her father, Anton Romba, were both Polish immigrants, who arrived in the United States about 1920. Dorothy's aunt had sponsored her sister Katherine to come from Poland. Dorothy's father had come separately with another large group. They had both settled on the north side

## The Shepherdess

of Milwaukee near Bremen Street and Concordia Avenue. Dorothy related, "My aunt found out that my father had just come from Poland and told my mother about him. My mother replied, 'Oh, he's not my type.'" But meet they did. Not long after, they were married and had three children Helen, John, and Dorothy.

Dorothy was born on March 30, 1927. She recalled, "My father worked and dug ditches in Mequon to open up the pipeline for the telephone and gas companies. He would come home very exhausted. My mother would not expect him to do anything when he arrived home. She would make him dinner or a sandwich. He only worked from spring through the fall. In the winter he would be home with us. My mother had to make sure we had enough money to last us through the winter and, by golly, she did. She was an amazing lady and taught me how to be money-wise."

I asked Mom what her life was like growing up. She smiled and said, "It was a good life growing up. It was very simple. Every night we would go sit on the front porch and talk. Mom would give us a nickel for ice cream and we would run to Tompkins for our special desert treat. It was about three blocks from our house, and I would go with several of the kids from the neighborhood. That was the best part of our life and we *loved it*."

I asked her if her parents were responsible for her beliefs. She told me that, when she was a small child, her mom would take her by the hand and they would walk to Sorrowful Mother's Novena every Friday night at St.

Casmir's. "Being young, I really didn't understand it much," she said, "but I'm sure that the Blessed Mother must have been happy to see a child in attendance with her mother. Our family all went to church together every Sunday. It was really nice."

Mom attended grade school at St. Casimir's where she would eventually be married and then went on to Riverside High School. Dorothy's sister Helen met and married Ervin Bishop. They settled on Milwaukee's south side and had five children–Marianne, James, Patricia, Robert, and Thomas. Dorothy's brother John was employed as a government engineer who designed headgear to protect soldiers' hearing. This job precipitated his move to Aberdeen, Maryland, where he settled and met his wife Mary Jo. They had a daughter, Katherine.

Dorothy then recounted how she had met Ervin. "I was at the Eagle's Ballroom on a date with another fellow," she said. "His name was John, and he was attending the School of Engineering. He was a good friend of Dad's brother Gene. Actually they were roommates on the east side. John introduced me to Erv and Gene, who were there 'stag'. We chatted for a few minutes. The following week I got a call, 'Dorothy, this is Erv.' I said, "I don't know any Erv." He replied, 'I'm the guy you met at the Eagle's Ballroom on Sunday.' Erv, who attended Pulaski High School, was managing a movie theater. He asked me out. I thought to myself, "What have I got to lose? So, I accepted. We went out that Saturday and had a nice time. He insisted that we

## The Shepherdess

see each other the next day. Oh, he was really hooked right from the start!"

"So when Ervin came to meet your parents for the first time, how did that go?" I asked.

"Oh, I don't know. My parents were glad I was having fun and going out. I was already twenty-three."

"Did they like him at first?"

"Yeah!"

"What did they like about him?"

Dorothy continued, "My mom never really said too much. As soon as he came over we'd go out, to dinner and a movie. Oh, there is something that I must confess. We met in October, mind you. For Christmas Eve three months later he came to the house and pulled out a small box and said, 'Dorothy, will you marry me?' In the box was a beautiful diamond, but we had never talked about marriage before and I was a little bothered. I looked at him. I wasn't quite ready for that yet. No, I really wasn't. I felt bad for the guy. He had spent a lot of money on the diamond but I wasn't really ready. I've always had empathy for everyone. Sometimes too much empathy can be a bad trait, as you lose your sense of reality."

"How could Ervin afford it? Weren't diamonds expensive?"

"He had a good job. He could afford it. Diamonds were much cheaper then. However, I was still taken aback. Can you see my point?"

"How did your mother feel about you getting engaged

for Christmas?"

"She let me be my own person. She never tried to dominate us. She thought he was nice. A Polish Catholic? What more could she want for her daughter? Oh, mercy!"

"What would most mothers say today if their daughter was engaged so quickly?"

"Oh my gosh! Times are quite different these days."

She continued. "That spring we were planning our wedding for October. Erv was in the reserves. We chose October, as it is the month dedicated to the Blessed Mother. We were going to dedicate our marriage to the Blessed Mother for her greater honor and glory. Suddenly he was called into service, where he served as a medic in Japan for an entire year. While he was gone, let me tell you, we got to know each other quite well. He wrote me every single day. I didn't write that much, maybe every second or third time. He was hooked. He really was. During that year my mom became my best friend. We shopped and planned the wedding together. It was so much fun."

When Dad was in Japan, he sent Mom two very precious gifts–a beautiful, classic, eight-piece set of white-bone china with a gold rim and an exquisite necklace of cultured Japanese pearls. She has cherished both these gifts her entire life. Mom also told me that Dad surprised her with a trip to Florida for their honeymoon.

Home from Japan at last, Dad was looking for a job. Mom, working at the Perlick Company in the accounts-payable department, had an idea. She went in and talked

## The Shepherdess

to the head of personnel. Shortly after, Dad was hired and worked there the rest of his professional career.

Early in their marriage Dad would bring Mom roses for special occasions, and often for no special occasion. He would give her the flowers as tokens of his love. After a while Mom suggested he stop, since the cost of raising a large family was so high. Dad honored her request. But after the kids were gone, he reverted to his old, loving ways. Once again he would surprise her with bouquets of flowers to show his deep love.

Time went by. One day Mom and I broached the topic of the eleven kids. Mom said how truly blessed they were to have these wonderful children. Before their marriage, Mom had told Dad that due to her irregular cycles, it was possible that she might never be able to have any children. (I told her that was too much information!) Dad had replied, "That's okay, we'll just adopt some."

The prediction quickly proved wildly inaccurate. Just as in the Prayer of Jabez, Dorothy and Erv were ready to enlarge their territory. Enlarge it they did. Their dream of a loving family came to fruition with these wonderful gifts from God. "I always thought I'd like four children, two girls and two boys," Mom said. "I don't really know what happened. Well, I got my *two* boys." Mom gave all her baby items away after Margaret (the tenth child) was born. She just didn't anticipate having any more. Beth was definitely a surprise, but in hindsight, and as Mom put it, "A huge blessing from the Lord." I remember telling Mom that she had been pregnant for a total of eight years and four months (She was a month late with Frank). "Rick–only you would think of that!" she laughed.

Terry and I attended Our Lady of Good Hope each week, usually for the 5:30 p.m. Saturday Mass. Most of the siblings would attend this Mass, and we would all sit together. It was incredible to see all of them lined up like soldiers to make their way to church a few short blocks down the street. It was like a rerun of *The Sound of Music*, with Captain Von Trapp!

Several times I was invited to participate in family outings. Occasionally this included a rare treat, going out to dinner. Ponderosa, a local steak chain, was a favorite restaurant where Erv would take his family. Each member of the family could order their own special steak dinner. Other unforgettable meals included fish fries at the VFW Post and Wrens, two local favorite restaurants of Erv's.

Over time, I came to know the Bishop cousins, Dorothy's sister Helen's family. The two families would alternate home locations for each holiday and celebrate together. The Bishop family was quite tall. I distinctly remember Frank, Terry's brother, asking one of the boys, "How's the weather up there? At the time, Dorothy's mom, Katherine Romba, was living in the duplex above the Bishops. She was a wonderful woman who spoke with broken English reminiscent of her Polish heritage.

Of all the activities I did with the family, the nightly meetings with Mom were the best. She always said. "All

## The Shepherdess

day I work hard, run errands, so by the end of the day I'm tired–a perfect recipe for a good night's rest." At least four nights a week, Terry and I would arrive home and go into Mom's bedroom and there, on the edge of her bed, sit and talk. Often these chats lasted for hours. Mom typically retired by 8:00p.m., since her day always began at 4:30 a.m. We talked about everything under the sun. Mom's commonsense point of view was always right on target. She would have made an excellent counselor–she really was one, without the official title. Mom is truly the matriarch of the Wiencek family. A matriarch is, by definition, a woman who rules a family, clan, or tribe. Dorothy's rule can be likened to that of a shepherd caring in every possible way for her sheep. By sheer numbers alone, I would certainly classify the Wienceks as a tribe! I soon learned Mom's favorite saying, "Jesus, I trust in you." Each morning, she would without failure repeat a favorite prayer:

Jesus, Lord - I offer you this new day because I believe in you, love you, thank you for your blessings. I am sorry for having offended you and forgive everyone who has offended me. Lord, look on me and lead in me peace and courage to do your holy will and your humble wisdom that I may serve others all day. Thanks be to God!

Mom said that when she was short for time during the day, she would keep her prayers brief. "Jesus, Mary–I love you" or "Jesus Mercy, Mary Help" were two favorites.

One night Pat and Terry organized a girls' pajama party and invited me to partake for a short time. This gave me new insight, a glimpse into what it would have been like to have had sisters.

Yes, those were enjoyable times for all. But with such a large family, sometimes something *had* to go haywire. As one story goes, years before the family had gone one Saturday to Muskego Beach Amusement Park. They all loaded themselves into the 1965 red Chevy station wagon to make the trip. By late afternoon it was time to head back. They arrived home not only tired but one person short. They had left poor Paul at the park! Dad quickly called. Paul had been located. Dad drove all the way back to find Paul wholly unfazed, sitting with an older woman and eating an ice cream cone. After, Dad devised a buddy system to prevent this from ever happening again.

One morning, I was a bit late picking up Terry for school. As I pulled up in front of the house, Terry came running out. We pulled away and started off on our way. Suddenly we heard a scream. I braked, looked around. Had I hit anything, anyone? I heard another scream and glanced behind the car. There was Mom, chasing us down the street with a glass in her hand. "Rick!" she exclaimed, "You didn't have your orange juice yet!"

When a McDonald's was being built a few blocks from their house, the kids all grew excited. Now they could participate in the new fast-food craze much easier. However, for health reasons Mom didn't want the kids to eat too much of that food. As she spoke about it she would refer to the new establishment as "Muck-Donald's," which

## The Shepherdess

would get laughs every time. Sometimes the kids would mimic her pronunciation to get laughs of their own.

Tuesday, Mother of Perpetual Help Day, was Mom's special day of the week. As a young girl, she and her mother would walk two miles after supper each Tuesday to St. Gall's Church to attend the Mother of Perpetual Help (MPH) devotions. This prayer service asks the Blessed Mother to intercede through her son Jesus to answer prayers. This Mom did for ten years, until she married. She would recite the Memorare, a prayer to the Blessed Mother. "The Blessed Mother asks us to pray, pray, pray, and we do so each Tuesday," Mom said. Coincidentally, countless blessings have come through the years to the Wiencek family on Tuesdays, and one of Mom's favorite sayings is, "Everything good happens on a Tuesday!"

Mom once told me that her favorite color is yellow. "It's just such a bright and cheerful color," she explained. Her favorite number? Three. "The kids would always ask me to pick a number and I would always say three," she says. "I don't know, I always just *liked* that number." If I were a betting man, I would wager it just might have something to do with her respect for the Trinity–the Father, Son, and Holy Spirit.

Of all the family, the member I came to know least was Erv. He was usually gone–off to work. Erv was a supervisor in the electroplating department at Perlick Company. Nonetheless, all indications were that our relationship was about to change. Dad had one part of the basement fixed up with a couch, a chair, and a record player. It was "his" special place to retreat. The rest of the basement was relatively cluttered. Dad asked me to join him down there in an effort for us to get to know each other, a bonding of sorts. But as it turned out, we really didn't talk a great deal. We would start out chatting, but soon he would move on to his assortment of eclectic memorabilia and that would be the end of it. I felt as if I was being initiated into a fraternity. Nonetheless, these meetings became somewhat of a standing joke in the family. I remember Dad yelling my name from the basement one time. All the kids were laughing. "For a joke, I said to the kids, "No–not the basement– anything but the basement!" Regardless, I did eventually go down to meet and chat. Dad was a man of integrity and always had everyone's best interests at heart, including mine.

The Wiencek family had been in their house only since December of 1968. Previously they had lived on First and Chambers Streets, where they belonged to St. Elizabeth's Parish. The younger kids attended St Elizabeth's grade school. Chris, Terry, Pat and Mary were attending St. Joan Antida High School. Mom told me she was concerned about the girls, who used public bus transportation. There had been several incidents at the bus stops. "This is not a good neighborhood for these young girls," Dad told Mom. The situation was getting drastic. They needed to move.

At the time, Dad's company, Perlick's, moved its plant operations north to Good Hope Road. This made a move

## The Shepherdess

to that area quite attractive. But could they afford it? They looked for a house for six to eight months. Mom said special prayers. She recalls, "I prayed, Mother of Perpetual Help, you must find us the perfect house for all these children so that they will be happy and have a good family life. I promised Our Mother that I would put her picture in our living room for all the years that we would live in the house." Mom told me that on August 15, Christine was scheduled to attend Mass at the St. Joan Antida "Mother House" located in the town of Granville. That same morning, Mom noticed a newspaper ad for a house in the area. It was on the Feast of the Assumption that they found their new home. As they drove by, Mom remarked that she absolutely loved it, without even stepping inside. "I don't even need to go inside. We're buying it!" she told Dad. "Dad thought I was a "cuckoo lady," Mom said. Upon viewing, the entire family fell in love with the new house. "It met our requirements completely –$22,700, and a larger house with two full baths. It was close to church, and there was a Sentry grocery store down the alley, a block in back of the house. Furthermore, it was only ten minutes from Dad's job, right up Good Hope Road. What more could we ask for–Thank you, God!"

Becky was nine months old when they moved. The house was vacant when the family put in an offer. Each evening after work, Dad would stop at the house to paint until late each night, so the house would be clean and bright for his family to move-in late December, 1968. The move was scheduled for December 24, the day before Christmas. Mom moved into what she has always described as "the most beautiful house in the city of Milwaukee." The day of the move-in, all the kids pitched in. "They all put the house together beautifully–they were fabulous and worked as a team," Mom said. "We could have entertained that night." Later that day Mom went with one of the girls to purchase a fresh Christmas tree. They found a beauty. "Every step of the way was a blessing. MPH was walking with us. How could we fail?" Mom added. "Our very first Mass was on Christmas Eve at Our Lady of Good Hope. The church had been located in the basement of the school. This turned out to be the first Mass in the brand new church the congregation had just built. It was exciting and uplifting–quite a welcome to the new church. However," she goes on, "there was still just one thing missing. I hadn't kept my word to MPH. I had found the perfect picture of Our Mother, but I didn't have the money to pay for it. Terry, who had a job at Militzer's bakery, volunteered to buy it for the family. The Blessed Mother's picture has been sitting on that wall in our living room ever since."

The Wiencek family was led to greener pastures. Dorothy's prayer had been answered. Each Friday night the family would gather in the living room and carry on a tradition–to pray together to consecrate the family to the Sacred Heart.

Renewal of the Consecration of the Family

Most sweet Jesus, humbly kneeling at Thy feet, we

## The Shepherdess

renew the consecration of our family to Thy Divine Heart. Be Thou our King forever! In Thee we have full and entire confidence. May Thy spirit penetrate our thoughts, our desires, our words and our works. Bless our undertakings, share in our joys, in our trials and in our labors. Grant us to know Thee better, to love Thee more, to serve Thee without faltering.

By the Immaculate Heart of Mary, Queen of Peace, set up Thy kingdom in our country. Enter closely into the midst of our families and make them Thine own through the solemn enthronement of Thy Sacred Heart, so that soon one cry may resound from home to home. May the triumphant Heart of Jesus be everywhere loved, blessed and glorified forever! Honor and glory to the Sacred Hearts of Jesus and Mary! Sacred Heart of Jesus, protect our family.

How remarkable it was that the family had moved and joined Our Lady of Good Hope Church. There is no such thing as coincidence. The words "good" and "hope" would become their mantras for years to come. "Good" is a synonym of "superior," and "hope" of the word "wishes." The Blessed Mother had answered the prayers of this family, granting them a life far beyond their hopes and dreams–a wonderful stepping stone to a future filled with abundance. I have often wondered if "GOOD HOPE" had any significance as an anagram. If so, it might look like this:

| God | Omnipresent | Opportunity | Dorothy |
| Humility | Obedient | Perpetual | Ervin |

# Birk

As weeks turned into months, Terry and I were becoming serious. I was in love with not only her but her whole family. Somehow I had been especially blessed to find these wonderful people. Were they my replacement family? I remember hoping that my brothers might find similar relationships in their lives. John was scheduled to meet the Wiencek family a few days later. The family had invited me for Thanksgiving Dinner and had extended the invitation to include my brother John, who had nowhere else to go.

On Thanksgiving Day, 1972, John and I arrived late in the afternoon, to find the table already set. With its several leaves and an extra folding table appended, it extended far into the living room. We all gathered around. Erv and Dorothy led us in a beautiful prayer. Then Dorothy asked that we go around the table and each mention one thing he or she was most thankful for. The sentiments were beautiful in their simplicity. Each expressed heartfelt gratitude. Then we sat down—all fifteen of us—and enjoyed a wonderful meal with all the trimmings. Mom and the family had prepared the meal, which included several pumpkin pies. Since John hadn't had a home-cooked meal in months, he was in his glory. Long after everyone else had finished, John continued to eat. Mom brought him seconds and thirds of everything. She was thrilled to make him happy. The kids got a kick out of the "eating machine," but I remember being a bit embarrassed. Once again, the Wiencek family demonstrated generosity and graciousness. That night I

## The Shepherdess

thought to myself that if Terry had even half the qualities of her mother, I'd be the luckiest man alive. All indications were that she did.

Not long after, I received a letter from Linfield College, a small, liberal-arts school in Oregon, that I had been accepted. After a great deal of thought, I decided to transfer and play my final year of basketball there. I would be able to earn my business degree within seventeen months. But I would have to leave for Oregon just after the first of the year.

I knew that this was the best road for me, but leaving Terry and her family proved to be very difficult. I spent the holidays with the family, a very special time. In early January I loaded up my Volkswagen and after many sad goodbyes, started my trip. Dorothy had food ready for my drive and assured me that she would pray for my safety. The trip was very emotional, and offered extensive time for soul-searching. I knew that Terry and I would be together soon. I didn't know exactly how, or exactly when. The details and divine timing would be up to the Lord.

# Patricia Ann

*Patricia, the third-oldest child, was born on December 2, 1954, and entered the heavenly kingdom on March 9, 2006. She was named after St Patrick's Day, a special festival day Dad loved. From early on, the family would always kid Pat about her height. Each year for thirty-four years I would surprise Pat with a telephone call just before Christmas. Each year I would ask her if she come over and put the angel on the top of our tree, since no one else could reach that high! "Rick—you got me again!" she would laugh. Now I call Katie, her daughter, for the honors, to carry on the tradition.*

### Pat's favorite Prayer to the Holy Spirit

Lord Jesus, I give you my heart for it is yours. I give you my soul for you are mine. Take my hands that they may be used for Your Greater Honor and Glory Lord. Now and forever! Amen.

The trip to Oregon was a long one. The weather was inclement. Nevertheless, I made it there safely. I went the southern route through Salt Lake City to visit a friend at the University of Utah because the weather was less treacherous on this route. However, I did encounter snowstorms along the way. I finally arrived in Bay City, Oregon, located on the Pacific Ocean. It was great to see my parents and grandparents again. School would start within a week. Just like Erv and Dorothy, Terry and I corresponded

## The Shepherdess

by letter several times a week. Surprisingly, I even got several letters from Dorothy. I missed Terry and the family very much. At times I wondered if I had made the right choice. School was going well. I had a pleasant roommate. But after many long conversations with Terry on the phone, I asked her to marry me—on a Tuesday night. She accepted. We decided to marry in March, the only break we had. We were ecstatic. Our wedding would be spectacular.

On March 17, 1973, Ervin drove Terry to church in the red station wagon, a tradition that would be carried on for all the girls. It was a typical cloudy and windy March day. Terry's sister Chris was the maid of honor. My brother John was the best man. The attendants were Pat, Mary, my cousin Jack, and my high school friend Dave. Dorothy sewed Terry's bridal gown as well each of the bride's maids dresses, in a lovely shade of spring green. My parents had driven all the way from Oregon. Unable to attend due to his Navy responsibilities, my brother Tom called us on our wedding day from Spain.

The Mass at Our Lady of Good Hope Church was beautiful and went flawlessly. Afterwards, the wedding party drove to the hospital to visit Terry's grandmother, who was an in-patient. We went into her room clad in our wedding apparel, to share our wedding day with her. We showed and told her how important she was to the family and how much we all loved her.

I remember Mom telling me how happy she was that I was now part of the family. She welcomed me without reservation. She also told me that I was her best-looking son-in-law. Since I was the only one, it got a big laugh. That day the Lord blessed me with this wonderful bond. Erv and Dorothy paid for our honeymoon, a week of lodging in Milwaukee. What had been planned in less than two months came off in spectacular fashion. The Blessed Mother had intervened in our time of need. All our prayers had been answered.

The week went by quickly. I flew back to Oregon while Terry stayed in Milwaukee to finish school. We would finish our semesters by early May and Terry would fly out to join me. The weeks seemed like a lifetime. Meanwhile, my mother and I found a beautiful apartment on the edge of the Portland State campus. I had a summer job lined up at a Portland freight company for some fifty-six hours a week. Soon after she arrived, Terry quickly whipped our apartment into shape–she was so well organized, just like her mom. Within a short time, we started receiving little care packages from Mom–towels, quilts, linens, and religious items that helped us to decorate our "first home." These packages, Mom's gifts of love, would continue through the rest of our marriage.

Shortly after, my brother John moved to Oregon. He took a teaching job at a community college and lived with my parents on the coast. Tom's Navy tour was ending and we were all excited to see him. Soon the whole Birk family would be together again, this time in Oregon. Free at last, Tom and his girlfriend Carolyn drove from Rhode Island

## The Shepherdess

to Oregon, where they too eventually settled. On the way, Tom and Carolyn stopped to meet Terry's family. They had a wonderful dinner and a great time with all the kids. Tom was very impressed with the family, their generosity and graciousness. He was most impressed by–"in awe of"– Dorothy, whom he called one incredible woman.

At the end of the summer, Terry took a job in a bank, where she worked until her acceptance by the University of Oregon nursing school, which she entered the following fall. On March 9, 1974, Tom married Carolyn in her hometown of San Diego. I served as the best man. In May, I graduated and went back to the freight company full time. Terry returned to school in the fall. With some eight weeks completed, Terry's class celebrated its "capping," a ceremony where each member received her esteemed nursing cap. Dorothy flew out for five days. It was a marvelous reunion. The candle-lit ceremony was emotional and memorable. Mom's presence was a wonderful gift. We were blessed that Mom was able to share in celebrating Terry's achievement.

On June 1, 1974, Christine married Kip, a ROTC member in college. Terry flew back to Milwaukee to act as Matron of Honor. Unfortunately, I couldn't get off work to attend. Over the next several years we were fortunate to have Pat, Kate, Mary Beth, Claire, and Carol each visit us. In December, 1976, Terry graduated with honors from the University of Oregon and accepted a nursing position at the University Hospital in the neonatal intensive-care unit.

In April, 1977, we learned that Terry was pregnant and due in December. On September 17, 1977, Pat graciously accepted Joe's hand in marriage. Joe was a computer-science graduate of the UW–Milwaukee. His family resided only a few houses down the street from the Wienceks and were also members of Our Lady of Good Hope. Terry and I went back for the wedding. Terry was now six months pregnant. With both of us graduated from college and working, we started looking for houses in the greater Portland area. We just couldn't seem to find the right one. Something seemed to be missing.

On December 12, 1977, we became the proud parents of a baby girl, Nicole Marie. I remember thinking about what Dorothy had said years earlier that children were a blessing–a gift from God. We were now experiencing first hand what she had said. Since she was the first grandchild on both sides of the family, Nicole received a great deal of attention.

In the past few years, I had taken an additional forty-five credits of accounting and finance courses at Portland State University. Terry and I had talked about moving back to Milwaukee and the opportunity to finally start an accounting career there. I knew how much Terry missed her family. We knew the timing was right; if we moved then, we would be able to see them all grow up.

We gave notice on our jobs. In the middle of May, we left for Milwaukee driving a U-haul truck, pulling our car behind. As the three of us made our way up the I-5 freeway towards Seattle, my parents pulled up alongside to wave goodbye. I remember the tears streaming down my mother's cheek as she made her final wave. It would be the last time I would see her healthy, for she would be diagnosed with cancer the following January at age fifty-nine.

Our trip back to Milwaukee was not without incident. Moving at a snail's pace, we made it through beautiful, mountainous Coeur d' Alene, Idaho in a hailstorm. Then in Nebraska the truck started wobbling as if it we had a flat tire. I stopped on the side of the road and checked, but everything seemed fine. We continued on, but the wobbling continued. I pulled over again—and this time noticed a six-inch chunk of tire missing. Here we were, stuck, with a spare that we couldn't use unless we removed most of our cargo to lessen the weight. Less than a mile from an exit, I decided to cautiously take the exit. God shined down on us that day. Right past the exit, we couldn't believe our eyes as we spotted a U-Haul dealership. Divine providence at its finest! With a large truck lift they were able to change the tire in thirty minutes without any unloading—as we enjoyed a leisurely breakfast. Yes, a guardian angel was watching over us. Thank you, Lord!

Our arrival prompted a big family reunion. It was wonderful to see the entire family again. Everyone wanted to get to meet and hold the newest member of the clan, baby Nicole. With Mom's help, we found an apartment only two blocks from the family home. Terry got a job in the obstetrics department at St. Michael's Hospital.

We joined Our Lady of Good Hope Church and settled into the community. In an effort to retire the church debt, the church had started a program whereby parishioners could lend the church money and be paid back in a lottery fashion sometime in the next five years. We took part and as a result had real ownership in the church. It was a smart move by the church, one well received by the congregation. The Wienceks would tithe each week and make a generous contribution. Terry and I did our best to follow their footsteps and share with the Lord. Each year the parish would have a sermon devoted to tithing. It reminds me of a humorous anecdote. At the end of his homily a priest announced, "For the offering tonight, we're going to do something different. Please take out your wallets. Hand them directly to the person behind you. We will let that person determine what you shall give." The congregation sat by, stunned. After a moment, he added, "I was just kidding. But it makes you think, doesn't it?"

It took me several months to find an accounting job, but on the plus side, I was able to take care of, and bond with Nicole. Soon Pat and Joe welcomed their own addition– Andrew Joseph, born on September 19, 1978. Now there were two grandchildren. During this period I spent a great deal of time with the family and got to know each one quite well. Before long, I landed a job as an assistant controller at a paper company. I felt extremely fortunate to be offered the position, since it was actually a step above my qualifications. It was at the St. Regis Paper Company,

## The Shepherdess

that I would meet another change agent in my life.

Wally Steitz, the company controller, spent hours teaching me the hands-on world of accounting, how businesses *should* be run, quite different from most of my coursework. Wally was an incredible individual with great integrity. He helped me more than he will ever know. It was at this time that I learned that my mother was quite sick and undergoing chemotherapy. On the evening of May 30, 1979, we got some shocking news. My mother had passed away. That night Terry gave me something to help me sleep. As she lie there with me asleep, she noticed a bright light-blue cloud of light circle over my head for some thirty seconds, a light that seemed to caress my head. She strongly felt my mother's presence.

My mother had died of cancer less than five months after her diagnosis. She had always been my rock, and it was an extremely difficult time for me. The three of us flew back for the funeral. Marjorie June Birk was laid to rest in Bay City, Oregon.

Now Dorothy would play an even more important role in my life. Not only would her wisdom and faith continue to shape our families beliefs in our Creator, but she would now become my surrogate mom. I specifically remember her explaining to me one day why it is important to show kindness toward everyone. Each day we are in the presence of the Lord in all we say and do. When we meet a new person, talk to a waitress, drive on the street, or go to work, we must act as if the Lord is at our side—because indeed, He is. We must show love and kindness just as the saints have, as shown by their examples. I asked her why she enjoyed reciting the prayers of the saints, and she said, "The saints are intercessors with Jesus. They will intercede for you if you need something bad enough."

Terry and I found a house on Mother's Day and purchased it on Father's Day. Now we had our own little nest and Nicole had a beautiful yard, full of trees to play in. I remember putting Nicole to bed each night and suggesting to her to dream of a "candy tree." Once you plucked a piece of candy, another immediately appeared. You would always have a lifetime supply and, consequently, would always have abundance in our lives. Nicole has always believed in that tree, and, as a result, has been blessed with riches and abundance.

Mom helped us decorate our new home and made several quilts for our family. Her role, I realized, was expanding. She had her own children aged eleven to twenty-six, some working, some in school, several living at home, each in many activities, and a few married, and now she had two grandchildren. Yes, her role continued to evolve, to accommodate all of our ever-changing needs. Career counseling? Parenting? Home decorating? Dealing with life's everyday ups and downs? She also became an expert with pillows, drapes, comforters, and quilts. These new tasks were added on top of her already heaping duty list. As usual, she welcomed these additional tasks as another way to serve. Her intrinsic gift of giving had been a family constant. Somehow Mom always seemed to rise to the occasion, to provide whatever was needed at any given time. Just as the Lord demonstrated to us, Dorothy always has the perfect recipe to best help and serve others.

People followed and listened to Jesus because He protected them. He fed them, healed them, and counseled them. When they were lost, He would seek them out. This is an example of a relationship that is built on trust. At times, we must submit and heed authority, and trust that our best interest is the objective. Jesus listened to everyone, even those who opposed him. He gained respect by submitting to his Father in Heaven, by suffering and dying on the cross. Throughout, he exercised forgiveness, healing, understanding, and compassion. He showed us the way with examples such as prayer, help for the less fortunate, the Eucharist, and, most of all, forgiveness. As Jesus entered Jerusalem on his final days to celebrate the Passover Feast, he rode upon a donkey. His presence on a donkey, as opposed to a horse, signifies that Jesus came in peace and openness, not in defiant opposition. He demonstrated peace throughout his suffering and crucifixion, when He became the Paschal Lamb, sacrificed for the sins of the world.

In John 10:11 Jesus proclaims, "I am the good shepherd. The good shepherd lays down his life for the sheep." In Chapter 34 of Ezekiel, the Lord points out the duties of the shepherd. The duties include tending to their flocks, keeping them from sickness and starvation, from being scattered or lost, and ruling them without force or cruelty. Like a shepherd, Dorothy watches over her family in the same manner, with a strong sense of personal honor. Life hasn't always been easy, and many difficult decisions needed to be made along the way. Time after time, with the grace of God, she continues to step up to the plate and shine.

A story comes to mind. A dad took his ten-year-old to his job on "Bring your son to work day." The trip meant taking the subway from $111^{th}$ street to $104^{th}$ street, changing to another subway, and finally a five-block walk. They arrived at 8:00 a.m. By 10:00 the boy said he was ready to go home. His dad said that he had to stay the whole day but, if he wanted to leave, he would have to make the trip home by himself. The boy, a little afraid, finally decided to make the trip. Being a little nervous, he almost missed the transfer to the second subway. He finally got off the subway relieved and thought to himself, "Thank God I made it!" Just then, his Dad came walking up, beaming with pride and said, "Great job, son!" He had followed him the whole time, watching from the next subway car. He was pushing his son out of the nest, but kept a close eye on him, monitoring his progress along the way.

Dorothy constantly gave us the courage to take that next big step in life, but would always be there for additional support. She has lent her help for years, unconditionally. She supports not only her family but her community as well. Being a Christian means treating others the way we want to be treated. For years Reverend Fred Rogers in his program *Mister Rogers Neighborhood* daily taught children

## The Shepherdess

a vital message. "Won't you be my neighbor?" he asked, simply. He endorsed the idea of living in harmony with everyone.

We can lend our neighbors strength with our love, joy, cooperation, and consideration. A family moving into a neighborhood generally can't choose its neighbors. This creates an opportunity for everyone to learn the art of blending characteristics and values, of accommodating everyone's uniqueness in order to live in harmony. This is a time when love and caring build relationships and increase community strength.

I have wonderful memories of the neighborhoods that I grew up in, amid families of varying ethnic and religious persuasions. These differences didn't prevent us from forging common threads to help our relationships mature and grow. Mom has embraced this philosophy throughout her life. If we as neighbors love one another, she believes, we can celebrate our similarities as well as our differences. Valuing her neighbors, she is loved and appreciated by these same people. She sees neighbors as another wonderful gift from God.

As I spent more time with the family, I came to know many of their friends. I noticed how Mom places great importance on the value of surrounding oneself with morally upstanding friends. She feels strongly that the people you associate with serve to mold you into who you become. Mom was always cognizant of her children's acquaintances. "Ninety percent of my friends are from our church community," she told me. "They are dynamite people. If you ever need anything, they are there."

Through the years Mom and Dad have had some terrific friends and neighbors–the Carrolls, Webers, Borowskis, Brennans, McMurtrys, Hills, Schroeders, Nabers, Whittles, Kohls, McGoverns, and Romanos, to name a few. Dr. and Mrs. Kenwood were members of Our Lady of Good Hope. Dr. Kenwood practiced at St. Michael's and worked with Terry for more than thirteen years and became the pediatrician for many of the family's grandchildren. A soft-spoken, kind, caring, dedicated doctor, he would even see patients at his home at any hour of the day, if necessary.

Without a doubt, however, Dorothy and Erv were closest to Bob and Theresa Bergs, also members at OLGH. The friendship started early at St. Elizabeth Parish. Initially, the Bergs were one of five couples in the Christian Family Movement. They had moved into the 43$^{rd}$ and Good Hope area a year earlier, only a few blocks from the Wienceks' new home and, surprisingly, were members of Our Lady of Good Hope church. An added bonus to the Wienceks' move was the rekindling of their friendship with the Bergs and the re-sharing of faith. Mom told me, "When Theresa bakes, she always brings something over. Any issue or any jam that I'm in, she's always there to listen. They are beautiful people. They don't make them any better than that!"

Always positive, Mom sees the best in everyone. Everyone, she believes, has some good qualities. She invites anyone and everyone into her home. When it comes

## The Shepherdess

to reading people and assessing character, she seems to have a sixth sense. I heard an interesting story a few years back about how things aren't always what they seem.

A priest assigned to a community church was walking down the street for the first time. A woman walked past and said "Hello." A minute later some parishioners approached and told the priest not to involve himself with her, as she was a prostitute. The next day he saw her again. She invited him to lunch. After some hesitation, he decided to go. When he arrived, she greeted him and invited him in. Together they walked into the kitchen, where he was greeted by a group of nine people eating a warm meal. Each day, he learned, she had been feeding the community's poor. She reminded him, "It's been very difficult to get a job in a town with a 60% unemployment rate."

"Never judge a book by its cover," is wise advice, and can certainly apply to our associations and relationships with others. Christians know that even a sinner can become a saint. God has prepared a table where saints and sinners meet as friends; a table where saints realize they are forgiven sinners and sinners realize they can become saints through God's grace. I've always felt that a person's character is a more accurate indicator of who they are, rather than their reputation. Your character is the essence, the core of who you are; your reputation is merely what others think of you. Throughout one's lifetime it takes great character to make unpopular decisions. Living your life successfully requires courage. The goals and dreams you seek require courage and risk-taking. You can learn a great deal from a turtle–a creature that makes significant progress only when it sticks out its neck!

The Lord used parables to teach lessons and to plant His seeds of wisdom in us. This is similar to a farmer who readies his crop with the harvest in mind. In early days before the plow, people hand-tossed and scattered the seeds and hoped for a successful crop. The plow vastly improved the success rate. We too, need to find more evolved ways of understanding God's word through better listening and vision. The huge turtles in the Galapagos Islands lay their eggs once each year. At this same time a large number of birds converge to feed on the turtle eggs. Some strong, young turtles break from their eggs and make it to sea. Others don't. Just as each young turtle fights for its single opportunity for survival, we must each be ready to hear and heed God's word at all times. We must be prepared for the opportunity when it presents itself.

# Mary Beth

*Mary Beth, the fourth-oldest child, was born on December 31, 1955, and reborn into everlasting life on April 16, 1998. She was named after the Blessed Mother. In the summer of 1979, I was driving up Villard Avenue on a very hot, sunny day. As I waited at a stoplight, a car pulled up next to me. I looked over to see a gorgeous brunette with large sunglasses, dancing to the beat of the music in her car. Our eyes met. She smiled at me, blew me a kiss. Stunned, I quickly looked away. As the light changed I looked back at her. She rolled down her window and raised her sunglasses from her face. "Nice try, Ricky!" Mary laughed and sped away.*

## Memorare

REMEMBER, O most gracious Virgin Mary, that never was it known that anyone who fled to thy protection, implored thy help, or sought thy intercession was left unaided. Inspired with this confidence, I fly to thee, O Virgin of virgins, my Mother; to thee do I come; before thee I stand, sinful and sorrowful. O Mother of the Word Incarnate, despise not my petitions, but in thy mercy hear and answer me. Amen.

Marking the next thirteen years were change, growth, and progress. Everyone was working hard and advancing down his individual path. The kids were growing. Little Becky, already eleven, was

## The Shepherdess

an excellent baby-sitter. Christine graduated from the UW-Milwaukee with a degree in primary education. She and Kip, an Army Officer and fellow graduate, were stationed in Panama, with Christine teaching in a grade school at their post. Pat and Joe moved to Illinois, where Joe took a job in computers. Mary Beth graduated from Marquette University with a nursing degree in 1977 and worked at St. Michael's Hospital with Terry. Kate, a dental hygienist, worked near Bay Shore. Frank graduated from Custer High and took a job with a friend in the concrete business, working long, hard hours. Claire, who had graduated from Custer High a year after Frank, was an elementary-education major and freshman at Carroll College in Waukesha. Carol, a senior at Custer, was on the cheerleading squad and the tennis team. Paul, a sophomore at Custer, was on the football team. Margaret (a.k.a. Terry's twin) was a freshman at Custer and a cheerleader as well. Finally, Becky was a fifth-grader at Our Lady of Good Hope grade school. She acquired cheerleading skills from her siblings and was on the grade-school squad.

Mom had stressed the importance of diligence and working hard. She encouraged everyone to try their hardest and to do their best every day. That most of the children pursued higher education was no surprise. Mom told me that she and Dad had always urged such. "We knew that college would be a real plus even though the children would have to pay for it on their own," she explained. "We felt that going on to school would definitely put them ahead.

We didn't have much in the way of funds, but the next generation should somehow be just a little better. What the kids accomplished makes me so proud."

She elaborated. "One day Frank, in his senior year of high school, told me he didn't want to go on to school. He had been offered a position with a concrete company where he could learn to handle big machinery. I told him that he was much like my father, a hands-on person. I told him, Frank, it sounds like it should work out just fine, and it did. He was very good at this position, and it did lead to bigger, better things later on. He would never have been happy working behind a desk. Paul has a different makeup, more like Erv. Give him a pencil and paper and he'll be a fine accountant or businessperson. Both boys, each with unique abilities, are doing just fine. Now Paul takes care of my books and Frank helps me with any home repairs and maintenance. I love it. That's how the Lord has always provided. He's always watched over me–Graces all the way through. I keep saying, Thank you, Lord. Thank you Lord! You're so good to me."

It was all too clear–this family's humble beginnings had laid the foundation for future success. I firmly believe that a person's desires and purpose are instrumental in shaping one's life. Defining and focusing on a specific intent constructs a path for attainment. Seemingly, each child had this strong sense of determination to find his or her own path in life. Circumstances that many feel are determined by chance, are actually created by these same

## The Shepherdess

strong intentions, a product of upbringing and environment. The power of positive thinking combines with the law of attraction to construct reality. As I reflect, I can express this all-important equation by the following: "Cost of the Wiencek home–$22,700. Square feet/person–118. Number of TVs–one (14-inch black and white). Upbringing–Priceless."

Mom has always been proud of her children, as any mother would be. She is most proud that they have all grown into solid Christian people and have forged their own ways. I remember a story of four ladies bragging about their sons one day. "My son is a priest and he is very respected in the community," said the first. The second said, "My son is a Bishop; revered by all." The third replied, "My son is a Cardinal–referred to as "Your Eminence." The fourth smiled. "My son is six-foot-eight and weighs 280 pounds," she said. "When people see him coming, most say 'Oh, my God!'"

Since I was fortunate enough to have had a scholarship for basketball, I felt a calling to do some volunteer work. The timing was ideal. The fifth-grade-basketball coaching position at Our Lady of Good Hope opened up. It was exciting to work with the young boys. Never having coached before, I found myself with eighteen enthusiastic, energetic fifth-graders. Like any teacher, I wanted to give them valuable information, and teach them proper fundamentals. I kept this group for four years, through eighth grade. The team made significant progress and enjoyed much success. It was an added bonus that this was Becky's class. As a cheerleader she attended all our games. It was fun to share the adventure with her, and her squad made a huge difference for our team.

Wisconsin has its share of harsh weather, and summer gives a family the best chance to get together outdoors and celebrate. For the Wienceks, this meant picnics on Memorial Day, Labor Day, or the Fourth of July, usually at Brown Deer Park or Doctor's Park. These were what Mom referred to as "the best of times." Summer was Mom's very favorite time of year. "The kids would run around and everyone would bring their favorite dish of food to share. It was a whole day spent in the park with the family. It just couldn't get any better," she would say. There was not only great food but fun activities. The girls would show off their latest swimsuits. Many of the siblings would bring friends or even potential spouses. There would always be a volleyball game and a chance of a softball game as well. A hike through the trees, down to Lake Michigan, only a short distance away brought everyone even closer to nature. By late afternoon the grilling was complete, and we would all partake of a wonderful feast." Since Mom didn't have to get the kids onto the bus for school, this time of year was far less stressful. "The summers were a little more relaxing," she put it. "The kids had their part time jobs. It was really good."

Mom told me that she also loved their small plastic above-ground backyard pool at home. She was talking literally from experience. "One time we came back from an outing, and the kids picked me up and dumped me in the pool," she recounted. "I couldn't believe it! I was angry and laughing at the same time. But I was just fine by morning."

A trip to Milwaukee's Fourth of July fireworks was a must. The celebration, held right on the Lake Michigan shore, provided a spectacular view. To get a good seat, one had to park at least a mile away and maneuver through crowds toting blankets and goodies. The firework display was always spectacular and well worth it, and the grand finale of fireworks was always very impressive. For years the whole family would attend together. As the kids grew older, friends would come along. As the family began to branch out into spouses and new homes, we would arrange to meet at a designated location.

On July 14, 1979, Kate married Tom, who lived only a few blocks away and was also a member of Our Lady of Good Hope. An accounting graduate from the University of Wisconsin, Tom soon became a C.P.A.

After only a year in Illinois, Pat and Joe moved back to Milwaukee, where Joe took a job with AT &T. They built a house in the northwest side of Milwaukee.

Once more God blessed our own Birk family. On December 17, 1980, we had our second child Jonathan Adam (gift of God). Jonathan was such a welcome addition. Our three-bedroom home was now complete.

On May 30, 1981 Mary Beth married Michael, a Natural Science major and graduate of St. John's in

Minnesota where he played on the water-polo team. Mike worked in the research lab at Johnson Controls. Later he would receive a second undergraduate degree, in Biomedical Engineering, from Marquette and then an MBA. The wedding was very festive. Once more Dad took out the '65 red station wagon, this time to drive Mary to church. Once again Mom, the official seamstress for all the girls' weddings, put her fine sewing skills to use. This time her efforts caught the attention of the *Milwaukee Journal*. A feature story the following winter, 'Wedding bells ring; Mom sews,' presented a full-page photo of the dresses at Brown Deer Park on that day. The photo highlighted Mom, Mary Beth, and her eight sisters–all bridesmaids.

Dorothy related to me, that as a child growing up her mother had been a talented seamstress. Her mother sewed *all* of Dorothy's clothes, including her wedding gown, and later sewed clothes for the grandchildren. When dresses were needed for a father-daughter dance in the late 1960s, Grandma was called upon once again. This time she was unable to help due to illness. This was the catalyst that started Mom's sewing legacy. On an old Necchi sewing machine at one end of the dining area she placed a small picture of the Mother of Perpetual Help, for encouragement. "I really didn't know how, so I'd put my picture of MPH right there and say, 'You really need to help with this!'" Such was the humble beginning of what came to be a lengthy sewing legacy.

Mary Beth had always loved Mom's wedding dress,

## The Shepherdess

so when the big day loomed near, Mary asked Mon if she could remake the gown she had worn some thirty years before. The remake, along with the addition of some 650 individually sewn pearls, was an enormous job. Adding eight bridesmaids' dresses made this a massive sewing project! The *Journal* reporter capped her article by citing Mom. "There's a standing joke in the family. Whenever some minor sewing tasks need to be done–sewing on a button, for example–Mom had the answer, 'I tell them, I don't do buttons, I only do wedding dresses.'"

It didn't take Mike and Mary Beth long to increase their family size. On February 18, 1982, they welcomed Brian Christopher into their family. If this wasn't enough, Pat and Joe had their second child, Katherine Ann, born on June 19, 1982.

After high school Carol decided to follow her sister Claire to Carroll College in Waukesha. Like Claire, she planned to major in elementary education. After a year at Carroll, she transferred to UWM and earned her degree. However, her experience at Carroll did give her a lifetime reward–a husband, Mark, an avid tennis player. Even though they went to different schools, they formed a lifetime bond. Mark graduated from Carroll with a business major and went to work for A.O. Smith Corporation. On July 28, 1982, Carol married Mark, and now has a lifetime doubles partner.

For several years Frank continued to work hard in the concrete industry. Having played the field for a number of years, he finally met his match, marrying Bonnie, from nearby Brown Deer, on October 16, 1982. Bonnie attended UW-Stevens Point and then received her business degree from Cardinal Stritch College. Not long after, Frank began to work for Happy Lawns, a firm owned by Bonnie's parents, where he has built a career and now oversees operations.

Claire graduated from Carroll in four years, but took something else from Carroll besides her diploma. Like her sister Carol, she met the love of her life–Jim, a member of the Carroll football team and student in the school of business. I remember attending one of Jim's football games at Carroll. At only 180 pounds, Jim played center and held his own, and then some, against an opposing line of far larger players. Jim went on to receive his MBA from UWM. On August 6, 1983, Claire accepted the hand of Jim in marriage.

With the kids growing up so quickly, Mom decided it was time to do more volunteering at church. Years before, Dad had asked Mom to consider doing so. Mom replied, "Erv, my mission and vocation is to be a good mother to all these children. I am not going to back off on that. Everything else can just wait." Already Dad was overseeing and bartending at the annual St. Patrick's Day festival–and serving as an usher as well. In the summer he called balls and strikes in an OLGH School softball league. Now Mom did start volunteering more. She served food at church festivals. Friday afternoons she breaded fish for the church's

## The Shepherdess

famous fish fries. She sewed many of the beautiful altar cloths and priest's vestments. A favorite job was opening the church and adoration chapel every morning. For years, rain, sleet, or snow didn't keep her from her commitment.

Mom loved giving of herself to the church, true, but if you asked her, she had her own very special "mission"– quilt-making. Through the years, Mom has made hundreds– if truth be told, probably thousands–of quilts. She makes and donates the quilts to church auctions, St. Vincent De Paul, and the Capuchin ministry in Detroit. Baby quilts went to Birthright. Her warm, colorful quilts adorned homeless shelters. One day, someone managing a shelter told Mom her quilts were so beautiful that people were taking them when they left. "That's ok!" Mom said. "It's so cold out there, if they need it, let them take it. I'll just make some more!" In short, anyone in need was a benefactor. Through the years she has made several quilts for each of her families and grandchildren, and each quilt is a cherished possession. "Every time I start a new quilt, I offer it up for the greater honor and glory of God," she told me. "There always seems to be enough money for material and batting." Her beautiful patchworks symbolize her unique ability to thread lives together with the fabric of God's holy grace.

Of all of Mom and Dad's church duties, the most incredible to me was serving as Lay Distributors. Just before Communion, the organ would start to play "Lamb of God "(Agnus Dei), and the Lay Distributors would walk to the altar to receive Communion. After, they would assist by distributing the body and blood of Christ in the form of bread and wine to the congregation. To see Mom and Dad in this capacity was quite uplifting. Their faith and piety sent a strong message to our family and the church family. Still today, every time I am at Mass and hear the Angus Dei I get goose bumps. I envision Mom and Dad walking to the altar and realize the impact they made on others.

Each Thanksgiving, Christmas, and Easter the entire family would convene at the Wiencek house. With the spouses, grandchildren, and potential spouses, the number had burgeoned to some twenty-five. Nonetheless, we all made room and enjoyed one another's company. These *were* the best of times.

Traditions were all-important. On Christmas Eve the family would gather and walk two-by-two, singing "Silent Night," to the nativity scene set up in the living room. Baby Jesus was lovingly placed in His crib to re-create His birth. Each year a different family member would have the honor. This celebration kept the meaning of Christmas intact. Jesus is the reason for the season. The ceremony complete, all turned their attention to the Christmas tree and the gifts piled beneath. This same tradition became a mainstay of many of the extended families.

One year Terry and I hosted an Easter brunch, another traditional family gathering. We assembled tables the entire length of our living room. By the time everyone in the family arrived, it was wall to wall people, but it was a

## The Shepherdess

wonderful, special feast. We realized the time and effort Mom had invested all the years cooking and baking to feed our hearts and nourish our souls.

On November 20, 1984, Mary Beth and Mike had their second child, David Michael Patrick. Within four months Pat and Joe had welcomed their third child, Christopher Joseph, born March 7, 1985. As if this wasn't enough, Kate and Tom had their first child seven months later. Sarah Kathryn came into the world on October 10, 1985. Soon Mark and Carol countered with their first, Lindsay Marie, born a month later on November 22, 1985. The family was truly expanding. Erv and Dorothy were the proud grandparents of nine, and they were only getting started.

With only three children at home, the house quieted down considerably. Mom missed the kids. Someone had always been there to drive her on errands. Now things were different. She wanted to visit the married children and see the grandchildren but had no way to get there. Everyone agreed; Mom would learn to drive. On her sixtieth birthday the family surprised her with a gift certificate for driving school. "I thought that the kids had all gone crazy!" she told me. "I really didn't want it and thought I had no chance of succeeding at my age. The children really loved the gift and thought it was perfect. I finally relented and gave it a try. When I took the road test the first time I didn't pass. Terry took me aside; gave me many lessons and gave me confidence. I owe it all to Terry. It has really been a pleasure to have the freedom to drive–it's been so wonderful!"

1987 brought two more additions to the family. Mark and Carol welcomed a second daughter, Megan Elizabeth on March 26, 1987. Paul, who had earned his business degree from UWM, had been dating Joy, from nearby Brown Deer. She was working on becoming a paralegal. It wasn't long before Paul decided "she was the one!" and asked for her hand. They were married on July 18, 1987. A few years later Paul received his MBA from Cardinal Stritch University and continues to work in finance.

The years 1988 and 1989 blessed us with three more additions. Jim and Claire had their first child, Steven Thomas, born February 11, 1988. Mike and Mary Beth had their third, Lauren Elizabeth, born June 30, 1988, and Tom and Kate welcomed their second daughter, Ashley Christine, on May 24, 1989.

With the number of children left at home dwindling, Mom would often find herself all alone. Even though she loved the family, she cherished her solitary moments when she could meditate and reflect. One night there came a pounding at the back door. Mom, home alone and already in her night gown, went to answer. She spied a large man at the door. He broke the glass, tried to break in. Luckily, Mom decided to run to her left through the living room instead of to the right to her bedroom. She raced out the front door and jumped off the front porch, tripping and spraining her ankle, but managed to limp to the Carrolls, a neighboring family. Within ten minutes the police arrived—to discover the thief in the garage, trying to steal the car. They chased him out the back and down the alley, and all the way to Brown Deer Park, where he vanished. I asked Mom about the experience. "I felt so violated and angry," she replied. "I was very lucky as I saw directly into his eyes through the window, and with the help of the Lord I persevered. Margaret had just sold her car the day before and $350 was on her dresser upstairs. He took that. He also took the house and garage keys." I asked her whether the insurance covered anything. "It covered the cost of changing the locks, but not the cash," she recalled. Margaret had sold her car to someone who was going to use it for a "demolition derby!"

Now there were only two daughters left at home, each with her own room upstairs. But this would be a short-lived luxury. Margaret had met Dean, a University of Wisconsin graduate and former minor-league player who was working in sales and marketing for the Milwaukee Brewers. It was not long before Dean popped the question. He and Margaret were married on October 28, 1989. Later Margaret completed her degree in elementary education from Cardinal Stritch University.

In the next year and a half, the number of grandchildren would reach sixteen. Mark and Carol added to their nest with their third daughter, Jennifer Katherine, born November 26, 1990. Jim and Claire welcomed a second boy with Thomas William on April 16, 1991. Finally, Frank and Bonnie were blessed with their first. On June 2, 1991, Matthew James came into the world.

And then there was only one! Becky was the lone child at home. This, too, would prove to be temporary. She had been attending UWM and dating. Then she met John and soon was off the market for good. A physics major, John had already graduated from the University of California-Santa Barbara and was a project manager with Sileno Company, Inc. On September 28, 1991, John and Becky were married. It was a beautiful day as Erv drove Becky up Rochelle Avenue on his final trip in the red wagon. Once again, but for a final time, Mom had made the dresses just as she had for all the other weddings. What did that mean to her? I asked, and she replied, "Oh, it was the best time ever. We would share. We'd all go shopping for the material and plan. Then we would go out to lunch on the way home from the fabric store. Those were the happiest times with the girls, planning and making the wedding dresses, the very happiest of times!"

Now all eleven children had been married at OLGH. Almost twenty-two years had passed since Mom had first prayed for happiness and a good family life for her children. Her prayers had been answered. MPH had provided for her and all the others far beyond Mom's wildest dreams. I asked Mom how she felt about having every one of her children married at one church. She replied. "Oh, it was the best. It was absolutely the best!"

For the past five years we had been vacationing for about two weeks each spring in Arizona. We'd leave cold, snowy Wisconsin to join my brother John in Scottsdale,

## The Shepherdess

Arizona, in the warm desert. It didn't take long before we fell in love with the climate and considered a home in nearby Scottsdale. With all the siblings married, the timing was right, we felt, and decided to make the move. Terry accepted a management position in nursing and I found a job in accounting.

In March of 1992, the entire family threw a going-away party–a fish fry at Thill Brothers in the Bay Shore Shopping Center. Everyone wished us well and gave us a warm send-off. It was a sad goodbye, but we were confident that it was the right move. We loaded up our belongings, put our faith in the Lord, and headed west.

# Kathryn Therese

*Kathryn, the fifth-oldest child, was born October 1, 1957. She was named after Dorothy's mother Katherine Romba. In college to become a dental hygienist, Kate had to provide her own patients for "cleaning and check-up" purposes. I volunteered and on occasion accompanied her to class. After our final session together, I called her instructor over. "This is the best cleaning and check-up I've ever had in my entire life," I advised him. Kate received an A on the assignment.*

## Prayer to Saint Catherine of Siena

God, You caused St. Catherine to shine with Divine love in the contemplation of the Lord's Passion and in the service of Your Church. By her help, grant that Your people, associated in the mystery of Christ, may ever exult in the revelation of His glory, Amen.

The trip to Arizona took three days. Jonathan and I drove in the truck with our household possessions and hauled our car along in the back. Nicole and Terry followed behind in our second car. On the first day, in St Louis, we encountered a huge rainstorm and nearly lost our way. It was raining so hard we couldn't see each other's car and had great difficulty following the road signs. Two days later, in Albuquerque, New Mexico, Nicole made one request—to eat at the "Big Texan," a steakhouse advertised prominently throughout the Southwest and known for its famous challenge, the "72-ouncer." Anyone who could

## The Shepherdess

finish the steak and all the trimmings in one hour would eat free. It was definitely not for light eaters. Knowing the reputation of my own hearty appetite, Nicole had assumed I would participate in the wager and end up with my photo on the wall. After reflection, I decided against it. My stomach was unsettled from the travel. Also, if I failed, the dinner would cost us a considerable sum and put us over our trip budget. Nicole was disappointed.

On our way across New Mexico and into Arizona the last day, we witnessed snowflakes. Who would have thought? To our astonishment the road to Flagstaff was closed to vehicles without chains. Our only alternative was to head south through the White Mountains, a four-hour trip that would prove a mighty test. Another storm bore down, this one with enough rain and sleet to force us to drive 15 to 20 miles an hour most of the way. Luckily, we couldn't see beyond the road, where parts of the road skirted deep mountain drop-offs. Only after hours of treacherous rain and sleet did the skies clear and before our eyes lay the Valley of the Sun–Phoenix. The temperature hovered in the 80s. The sun shone brilliantly. Welcome to Arizona!

We found an apartment only blocks from Our Lady of Perpetual Help, where Jonathan would attend fifth through eighth grade. When we took him to school, his classroom had room for only one more student. The only desk remaining was remarkably for a left-hander. It was … meant to be. We signed Jon up for baseball, an extremely popular sport in Arizona. Nicole finished eighth grade by correspondence from St. Eugene's back in Wisconsin and began to practice with the local Saguaro High School tennis team. In May, Nicole flew back for her graduation from St. Eugene's, where many members of the family attended and held a party for her.

In September of 1992, we found a house on McCormick Ranch, a mere mile and a half from Saguaro High School and three miles from Jon's grade school. It had a swimming pool and, of course, several sheltering palm trees. Our small homeowners association had its own tennis court–ideal for our family. My accounting job was but a few miles from our home. We joined St. Maria Goretti Catholic Church. Father Jack Spaulding, our new pastor, was not only well loved in the congregation but a favorite among the young people. Both Nicole and Jon acclimated easily. It was perfect. It all had worked out even better than we had hoped. Soon we were doing well, enjoying enriched, abundant lives.

Then came some stunning news. In October of 1992 Mom was diagnosed with colon cancer. The family prayed. When her surgery was successful, we all felt we had dodged a bullet. Later Mom told me, "I experienced a moment of truth when I was told I had colon cancer. Father Peter Carek gave me the Sacrament of the Sick and I was totally prepared to die. The surgery was scheduled on December 8 (The Feast of The Immaculate Conception of the Blessed Mother), and I thought the Blessed Mother would swoop me up and take me to heaven. Pat came to the hospital at 6:30 a.m. for encouragement and prayer. After surgery, I

## The Shepherdess

said to Pat 'What am I still doing here?' She said, 'Many important tasks are left to be completed and accomplished.' She was so right. As the kids bought their homes, I sewed all the window treatments and comforters for the beds. When this became too much, I resorted to making my quilts."

In 1993, the family welcomed three new members. Dean and Margaret were blessed with their first child, a boy, Benjamin Dean, born on August 23. Paul and Joy also had their first child, a boy as well. Timothy Jacob was born on September 9. Last but not least, Dana Catherine was born on November 22, 1993 rounding out Mary and Mike's family to two boys and two girls.

With Mom's recuperation, the family was once again in fine health. As I look back, I realized that no one in the family had ever been seriously ill before. We had been blessed in that regard. As the years went by, the family prospered and shared in life's daily graces. In 1995, Dean and Margaret had their second child. On May 10, Elizabeth Ann was born. Two months later, on July 29, John and Beth had their first child, Peter John. The grandchildren count was now up to twenty-one.

In February of 1996, we all received startling news. Mary Beth was diagnosed with breast cancer. Until now, we had been lucky. Mom's cancer had been removed. With the sole exception of Mom's sister Helen, a survivor, breast cancer had been absent. Mary Beth personally called each of her siblings to share her news. Her message to each was clear, "*Please* go get a mammogram now to make sure you're okay. Early detection saves lives." Terry recalls, "I will never forget the imploring quality in her voice." Mom was devastated by the sad news, but continued to pray fervently for a miracle to heal Mary.

After Mary had a mastectomy, chemotherapy, and radiation treatments, the doctors gave her a thumbs-up and were optimistic about her survival. Her hair began to grow back. She regained her strength. Soon she found herself back at work at St. Michael's hospital, doing the nursing she loved, ministering daily. She had a renewed spirit, a new lease, a passion to live life to the fullest and enjoy every moment. She also announced that she had a guardian angel. It was *true*, she told everyone, because she *saw* him. Now Mary, as we knew, always used superlatives. True to form, hers wasn't just a standard-issue guardian angel. No, Mary Beth's guardian was Raphael himself, archangel of healing. Mary insisted that she had seen him many times when she was sick and then recovering. "You are healed!" he told her, and her faith grew even stronger.

One day shopping (one of her other favorite past times), Mary came upon a beautiful oil painting of an angel. The painting seemed to call to her. She was mesmerized as she stared– how familiar! As she inspected it, she was convinced that this was the same Raphael who had kept watch over her while she had been sick. She told Mike about the painting. Mike went back to the store and then surprised her with the treasured gift.

## The Shepherdess

Mary Beth liked to decorate her home and let Mike do the cooking. Housekeeping, cooking, and baking were definitely not her strengths. Once, a parishioner asked her to bake cookies for a fund-raiser. Mary Beth replied with a quote to be echoed through the years, "Honey, Momma don't bake. Momma decorates!"

Mary Beth's real passion, however, was gardening. She would spend hours in her yard, planting annuals and perennials. Bayside Garden Center, a local florist and nursery, was her home away from home. Everyone at Bayside Gardens knew Mary and greeted her enthusiastically as she stepped foot into the greenhouses, choosing her plants and seedlings with care. Her gardens were spectacular and won acclaim, even gracing the cover of a local magazine. Mary Beth took great pride In her landscaping and sculptured gardens.

With Mary Beth's recovery, we were relieved. Life seemed to resume as usual. Blessings continued with three more children welcomed into the family. Paul and Joy had their second, Kristyn Danielle, on August 16, 1996. On May 16, 1997 John and Beth had their second son, Ryan Joseph. Dean and Margaret were blessed with their third child, Abigail Katherine, on July 17, 1997.

It was late in November that Mary Beth went back to the doctor, complaining of a backache. After a CT scan at St. Michael Hospital where she worked, Mary asked the technician, "How does it look?" He turned to wipe away a tear. Not one to miss a cue, Mary knew it was not good. She soon learned that the cancer had spread into at least twenty-seven sites in her bones.

Mary Beth and Mike were determined to combat the cancer. But after four months of chemotherapy and treatments, it grew apparent that the cancer was winning. Her days were numbered. Mary Beth and others discussed options, and agreed on home hospice. All the St. Michael's nurses pitched in to tend to one of their own. Mary's close friend Kelly organized a round-the-clock schedule of care. Nurses volunteered on their days off, and Mary found herself not the giver but the recipient of loving care. Kate regularly gave her "spa treatments," and brought along a wide selection of bright, cheerful nail polish for Mary Beth's special manicures and pedicures. Pat drove daily to Mary's house to pray with her before heading across town to work. Everyone pitched in. Once, Mary Beth's wig became so unruly that Kate was unable to style it. Kate took the hairpiece to her salon, where professionals trimmed and styled it to keep Mary looking as chic as ever!

The parish held a prayer vigil for Mary Beth. Friends and family rallied and pitched in with food, childcare, and home hospice. Despite being so debilitated, Mary Beth continued to call the shots regarding her healthcare. One day Kate heard her on the phone rescheduling her chemotherapy appointment to make the St. Eugene's dinner dance. "I'm going to dance my feet off!" she promised Kate. Though always the optimist, Mary Beth never made that dance.

## The Shepherdess

Terry flew back and served as a hospice nurse for a week. Mom brought Communion to Mary Beth each day and prayed with her. The painting of Mary Beth's guardian angel was brought to her bedside. Although she was losing strength, she said that she wanted to live until Easter, to go to Mass with the family on Easter Sunday. She knew Easter's message of the joy of the resurrection was so powerful. The generosity of others helped Mary Beth live her final days in peace. A product of her upbringing, she had come to terms and with faith accepted God's will. She asked friends to purchase cards for future special family occasions, cards she herself would not be able to personally deliver. On Easter, the family arranged for an ambulance to transport Mary Beth to church. Mike addressed the congregation, thanked everyone for the outpours of help and support. Two days later, on April 16, 1998, surrounded by loving family and friends, Mary Beth lost her battle.
The wake and funeral drew hundreds. Many stood in line for blocks to pay their respects. Mary Beth's brothers-in-law had the honor of being her pallbearers. Mary Beth had asked me to write a poem for her that Terry could use as her eulogy, and I was honored. It goes as follows:

### For Mary Beth

*Mary Beth was born on December 31, 1955, and was named after our Virgin Mother.*
*Her family was comprised of Mom and Dad, eight sisters, and two brothers.*

# Birk

*Mary Beth was a strong-willed child with an agenda of her own.*

*She loved sports and shopping and her stories were quite well known.*

*Our home was modest with eleven children, not much room to spare*

*We slept much like sardines, but we didn't really care.*

*The close quarters may have caused friction, resulting in some arguments.*

*Mary Beth, the strongest, was nicknamed 'Moose'. Staying away just made good sense.*

*Her tales of embellished stories are famous to this day.*

*An example, a 22-foot Christmas tree and a 16-ft. ceiling. What can we say?*

*Mary Beth referred to me as her surrogate mother or hero, as she would say.*

*I helped her with her reading and multiplication and comforted her during her nightmares, but she's my hero today.*

*St. Elizabeth Grade School, Custer High School, then on to Marquette,*

*Finally working for St. Michael's, when her education was set.*

*I was fortunate to work with Mary Beth on occasion, in intensive care.*

*So much of herself she would give, so much she would share.*

*Mary Beth was always as generous a person as you*

## The Shepherdess

would ever find.
She was caring and humorous, really a one of a kind,
Sometimes she "borrowed" items that ended up in her home.
I think it was the curiosity of how it would fit. Besides, it was just a loan!
Mary Beth's yard and her flowers were very important to her,
Undoubtedly that's why she was proclaimed Bayside Garden's number-one customer.
Mary Beth had a personal trinity- her family, nursing, and her belief in the Lord.
She juggled all three with a passion vigorously, and was never bored.
Even as she lie in her bed awaiting her eventual fate,
Her thoughts were of others–her children, her mate.
It would be very easy to become selfish at a time like this.
Her family, her friends, her home–so much she would miss.
Shortly after coming home from the hospital, Mary Beth said that she had found peace in her heart.
She said cancer is a humbling experience as it tears you apart.
It's strange that Mary Beth had a special love of angels for so very long,
Maybe it was a premonition, a feeling, or perhaps a need to belong?

*Her words seemed full of wisdom as she spoke towards the end.*
*It was as if God were speaking through Mary, a message he would send.*
*It's so very hard to trust that Mary Beth is better off today,*
*But we must trust in the salvation of the Lord in each and every way.*
*Yes, now Mary Beth is an angel, so we must not be sad.*
*Few are chosen for this station so early in life, so let us all be glad!*
*If one message from Mary Beth rings clear to me,*
*It's to love one another–love is the key!*
*I am thankful to the Lord for Mary Beth, and to the heavens I sing,*
*As I know Mary Beth's looking down, smiling, with her halo, waving her wing!*
*As Mary Beth looks down from heaven above,*
*I feel her presence, her soul, her love.*
*God loves us, Jesus died for us, the Holy Spirit empowers us, we've been taught,*
*But the mystery of faith is the real reason Mary Beth fought.*
*Easter, Easter, Easter was her goal!*
*It was the true meaning of Easter she wanted us all to know.*
*Death is just a transformation. There is no need to fear it.*

## The Shepherdess

*Jesus and now Mary Beth have risen from the dead,*
*transformed through the Holy Spirit.*
*This is the story that Mary Beth wanted us all to know.*
*The true meaning of Easter will help us all grow.*
*Right now I feel Mary Beth speaking through me,*
*She is telling everyone that Love, Love, Love is the key!*
*We love you, Mary Beth!*

Never were the strength, resolve, and deep faith of Mom and Dad more evident than at Mary Beth's funeral. One of the most devastating ordeals for any parent is the death of a child. The pain is indescribable. Their strength was a message to all that Mary Beth was now with the Lord and that God's will was done. We live our lives knowing that each day could be our last. The Lord took Mary Beth to heaven, where she is now with the angels. Always the joker, she left one last instruction for her final prayer service beside her crypt at Resurrection Cemetery. She had a banana delivered to her brother Paul, with a note, "I love you a bunch!"

The following spring Paul and Joy had their third child, Courtney Nicole, born on May 12, 1998. On October 22 Jim and Claire welcomed a daughter, Tricia Elizabeth.

To then add insult to injury, Kate had an abnormal mammogram in early 2000. After a biopsy, a specialist advised surgery. Kate was fortunate that her breast cancer was caught early and required only a lumpectomy. Still in its early stages, the cancer was contained. Follow-up included a mammogram every three months for a year.

Thank God, to this day Kate has remained cancer-free.

The following year John and Becky had their third child, a beautiful daughter to join her two older brothers. Elliana Catherine was born on June 30, 1999.

A year after Mary Beth died, a ceremony was held at St. Michael Hospital, and a tree was planted in her memory. In the fall of 1999 the American Cancer Association sponsored a luncheon focusing on breast cancer at River Hills Country Club. Terry, now a disease-management specialist, was the keynote speaker. We both flew back to Milwaukee from Arizona for the event. The luncheon would feature a fashion show, and the Wiencek sisters would serve as models.

Addressing the overflow crowd, Terry spoke from her heart. She told the moving story of Mary Beth's ordeal, of Mary Beth's journey from finding a dreadful lump to her untimely death. Terry described the dominos falling, setting off a chain reaction which caught us all off guard. Pat, too, she mentioned, had been diagnosed and because of mass diffusion had undergone a mastectomy. Only a few months before Mary's death, Terry herself had been diagnosed with early breast cancer, treated by a lumpectomy and six weeks of radiation.

In Mary Beth's case, the cancer's metastasis had caused system after system to fail, depriving her of the ability to use her hands and feet and causing blindness in her left eye. She had told the doctors that they would just have to keep experimenting with the chemotherapy "until you get it right!" She had had no intention of dying and leaving

## The Shepherdess

four small children. Praying hard, Mary Beth one night had experienced a visit from Archangel Raphael, the archangel of healing, who had told her she would be healed. We all came to learn that healing can take place on many levels– not just physically but, more importantly, spiritually.

In her address, Terry said that, five years before, she never would have guessed that this would happen. "We must be the poster family for breast cancer," she told an overflow crowd. She implored the audience to think of being "on the cover" and its effects on children, family members, and insurance needs. A prophylactic bilateral mastectomy may not even be enough; errant random cells may linger behind, causing cancer to form. The bottom line is that there are no guarantees. Terry cited advances in genetic testing and emphasized the importance of minimizing controllable cancer risk factors: smoking, lack of exercise, eating unhealthy food, and overusing alcohol. Again she urged the listeners to use good judgment, get annual mammograms, and do regular breast self-exams.

Last, Terry talked about happiness. "Happiness is a present that we can give to ourselves," she said. "Unhappiness is largely a function of how we relate and react to events in our lives. Overreacting to an adverse event only makes things worse. We each have the ability to give ourselves the gift of happiness. If you need some help, ask the angels in your life. So how do we survive breast cancer and other adversity? The answer is right in front of us. We must celebrate life by cherishing it and making the most of each day as it unfolds. Don't wait. Thank and appreciate all the important people in your lives. Remember, happiness is a state of mind and is here... right now! We love you, Mary Beth!"

# Frank Anthony

*Frank, the sixth-oldest child and the first of the two boys, was born on July 5, 1959. He was named after his grandfathers, Frank Wiencek and Anton Romba. At age twenty-six Frank volunteered to baby-sit our two children one evening. Terry and I finished our errands early and came home. Squeals of laughter came from the bedroom. Frank, Nicole, and Jonathan were all jumping on the beds, trying to see who could get closest to touching the ceiling.*

## Unfailing Prayer to St. Anthony

O Holy St. Anthony, gentlest of Saints, your love for God and Charity for His creatures made you worthy, when on earth, to possess miraculous powers. Miracles waited on your work, which you were ever ready to speak for those in trouble or anxiety. Encouraged by this thought, I implore of you to obtain for me (request). The answer to my prayer may require a miracle. Even so, you are the Saint of Miracles. O gentle and loving St. Anthony, whose heart was ever full of human sympathy, whisper my petition into the ears of the Sweet Infant Jesus, who loved to be folded in your arms, and the gratitude of my heart will ever be yours. Amen.

After Mary Beth's funeral, it was difficult to leave the family and return to Arizona. We seemed to be in a deep, depressing fog. Terry, especially, had a hard time getting over Mary Beth's untimely death and at the same time dealing with Pat's and her own cancer

## The Shepherdess

issues. Somehow, with prayer and time, we pulled together and found a way.

On February 9, 2000, Frank and Bonnie welcomed a daughter, Margaret Elizabeth. On September 14, 2001, John and Becky had their fourth child and third son, Charles Anthony. Now the "immediate" family totaled more than forty. With such a swift increase, Mom and Dad's house could no longer suffice, and local hotels, restaurants, and country clubs became the new venues for family holiday gatherings. With the distance involved, we were able to make only a few of these. I recall when I first heard of the change from Mom and Dad's house to a restaurant. It seemed so sad, the end of a long, time-honored tradition. From a practical standpoint, however, it made sense.

On October 6, 2001, Mom and Dad celebrated their fiftieth anniversary–an incredible day. A special Mass was set for Saturday morning. Family and friends honored the couple for the amazing accomplishment. After, a reception was held at Manchester Suites on Port Washington Road. Mom movingly thanked everyone for their love and support. She and Dad had requested that in lieu of gifts for themselves, that a donation be made for a new, larger crucifix for the church. Father Hying was dumbfounded when Mom presented him with a check for $1600.

Early in 2002, Margaret went in for her mammogram. The year before, she had learned of some questionable changes that her doctors wanted to keep an eye on. This year's mammogram showed the same–more questionable changes. She saw a breast surgeon, who scheduled a biopsy for April 1. When the biopsy indicated that she needed a lumpectomy, she felt it had to be some kind of dark April Fool's Day joke. To add insult to injury, the surgery was slated for April 16–the anniversary of Mary's death.

After the surgery, the doctor told her husband Dean that he was concerned. He was not sure that he had gotten "clean borders." A week later his suspicion was confirmed. He told Dean and Margaret that the cancer had spread. He recommended a bilateral mastectomy, with reconstruction surgery. The news hit hard, but Margaret courageously readied herself. Everyone was prepared for a long surgery, but not 17 ½ hours. The doctors performed the mastectomy and reconstruction procedures all at once. Recovery came slowly, over the next twelve to sixteen weeks. At the end of August, Margaret faced the next hurdle, four cycles of chemotherapy. Each cycle depleted her body even more, leaving her with low blood counts that called for further intervention. To regain her strength and flexibility, she was a regular at the physical therapy department. There on the treadmill 'frail, little Margaret' worked out next to burly men recovering from cardiac surgery. Challenges seemed to come from every direction. In early November, she was re-hospitalized due to a blood clot from her catheter. Soon the bills started rolling in. In addition to her health bills, additional charges totaling thousands of dollars came from a cell phone in Cleveland, Ohio. Yes, her identity had been stolen with her medical information!

## The Shepherdess

The year 2002 was quite the roller-coaster ride for not only Margaret and her immediate family but the family as a whole. Once again breast cancer had struck swiftly. True to form, Margaret had addressed the challenge just as had her sisters, head-on. Including Margaret, there were now five sisters who had been dealt that card. Today Margaret is grateful for the gift of her health and is our family's greatest breast-cancer success story.

On May 19, 2003, John and Becky were blessed with another daughter, Chloe Gabrielle. I remember asking Becky if she was going for the family record! On November 16, 2004, Paul and Joy had their fourth, a second boy, Adam Christopher, who brought the total of grandchildren to thirty-one. As of the first printing of this book, that sum is accurate. Stay tuned!

The families in Wisconsin had each purchased a home in the same general locale (within ten miles), mostly in the North Shore area of Milwaukee. The two exceptions were Pat's family, who resided in Brookfield, and we, in Arizona. This made it convenient for almost everyone in this close family to see one another, and it made it easy for Mom to visit each of her children.

Living in Arizona has its benefits. The weather is spectacular year round. In the past eighteen years since our move, many of the families had come to visit. Mom, a big sports fan, has come down several times and attended several Milwaukee Brewer spring training games, something she really loved. We took Mom to see the spectacular Grand Canyon. She thought the Grand Canyon was enjoyable, but she truly loved visiting Sedona, and all the red rock formations. Her favorite site in Sedona was "The Church on the Rock" – a very special Catholic church built to look like a big cross on the rocks and boasts a panoramic view of the area.

On June 12, 2005, after suffering for about a year with cancer, my dad passed away. I was able to fly up and spend some quality time with him a few weeks before he died. Our family flew up for the funeral. After a quiet, private service, he was buried next to my mom and grandmother in Bay City, Oregon.

By this time, almost nine years had elapsed since Pat and Terry had received their initial treatment, and both were getting regular checkups with their doctors. In January of 2006, just after the holidays, Pat went to the doctor, concerned that she "just didn't feel well!" Tests showed that Pat's liver was filled with cancer. Her breast cancer from seven years before had metastasized to her liver. Pat called us in Arizona with the news. She started with, "Terry, you are strong, aren't you? I've got some news and–I want you to be strong." Then she described what the doctor had shared with her and her prognosis, which was not good.

The doctor suggested a round of chemotherapy. The chemotherapy proved ineffective, as her cancer was now diffused throughout her liver. The doctor told Pat that he didn't think she would make it to Valentine's Day. Despite his prognosis, Pat prayed that she could somehow celebrate

## The Shepherdess

her youngest son Christopher's twenty-first birthday on March 7. Over the next few weeks she was in and out of the hospital several times. She wanted comfort, and all agreed that a home hospice would be set up. Family and friends surrounded Pat. Dad, Mom, her sisters and brothers and their families visited daily. Terry flew back to spend six weeks with Pat as her hospice nurse. Each day Kate and Margaret would come to visit and to assist. Mom had always said how much Pat calmed her spirit, and *now* Mom was coming each day to give Pat Communion and pray with her.

Like Mary Beth only a few years before, Pat wanted to be in control and planned her funeral in minute detail. The flowers, scripture readings, songs, individuals who would deliver a eulogy—were each personally selected by her. She even designed her own Mass card using a photo she had taken of her statue of the Blessed Mother gracing her front lawn. She added her private prayer to the Holy Spirit and painstakingly did the calligraphy of her own name as a final personal touch. Kate and Terry carried out her funeral wishes to the letter. I came back to spend a few days with Pat and help in any way I could. With Pat determined to go to church one more time, we made arrangements, and with the aid of a wheelchair Pat attended on Sunday morning. One night I asked Pat to name her favorite restaurant. She exclaimed "Yanni's." That night we surprised her with a takeout steak dinner and all the trimmings. Deeply touched, she insisted on coming to the table to share the family meal.

Sadly, after only a few small bites, she got sick and had to return to bed.

One of Pat's missions was to pray for and offer support for the seminarians. She knew there was a shortage of priests and wanted to offer her encouragement. She handmade each seminarian a birthday card and cards for special occasions. She prepared food and treats for them. She continued to pray for their welfare and hoped for someone to take her place and continue the cause when she was gone. Mom "received the torch" and even today perseveres in this mission in Pat's memory.

Shortly after Mary Beth had died, Pat on her way to work one day had asked the Lord to give her a sign of her sister. Moments later she spotted a license plate on the busy freeway, MBK RN. For the last two years Pat's spirituality continued to grow through her daily prayers and meditations. She lovingly recorded in a daily prayer journal her thoughts and messages from God and the Blessed Mother. She was told that she had been chosen for a calling of her divine heart. "I will never fail you! See Jesus in everyone," the Blessed Mother told her. Pat had asked the Lord to help her identify her mission. He had replied, "Your dream is my will for you," and continued, "My daughter, do not be afraid of what will happen to you. I will give you nothing beyond your strength. You know the power of my grace; let it be enough." In 2005 Pat had received a message in the St. John Vienney Adoration Chapel. The Lord said, "Come to me, my dear child, and I

## The Shepherdess

will help you grow into the image and likeness of my son. Your Abba." Viewing a Good Shepherd statue one day, Pat had heard, "All those that are lost shall be found." On Labor Day in 2005 she had told the Lord, "No matter how much you ask of me Lord, give me grace to do more." An answer had finally come. "It is I who has made a covenant with you." Four weeks later at church she had heard the following, "You have been chosen for a great cause. Believe in me and I will not fail you. Take hold of your principles and do not sway–hold firm. I am with you always. Your Savior."

In January of 2006, shortly before going to the doctor, Pat heard Jesus say, "*Come*, I have prepared a place for you! Let your light shine upon others as I have shined upon you." The Lord continued, "You have worked hard and your work is now complete. You will share in my joy forever." In the next few days Pat asked the Lord what would happen in her next life. The response, " I have desired you to do great deeds. You will be my spirit of light. Come to me, little child of grace, your days are numbered." The news from the doctor's office only confirmed these messages. Pat prayed on, and received her last messages just before entering hospice. "You will be used to fulfill My plan. Fear not, I am with you. I love you with all my heart. I will be using you for great things you are totally unaware of. Leave in peace! Come to me and I will shower you with blessings you never imagined possible. I am the Lord your God." One day after chapel the last message came. As she paused at the statue of the Blessed Mother, Pat heard, "Jesus is waiting for you. His plan has been fulfilled through you. I am with you always."

On March 9, 2006, two days after her son Christopher's twenty-first birthday and in the company of her loving family, Pat died. God had answered her final request. She, in turn, had answered His. She was now in His loving arms for eternity.

Pat's wake, like Mary Beth's, was attended by very many people. The receiving line, I remember, took over three hours to complete. Pat had touched the lives of many, many people. On the day of the funeral, a beautiful quilt that Mom had made depicting the Blessed Mother and angels was placed atop Pat's casket. Her brothers and brothers-in-law served as pallbearers. With input from virtually everyone, Nicole, Terry, and I put together a eulogy, which Terry presented at her service.

*"Patty Cake"*

*What do I remember about Pat? Her favorite color was yellow. Her favorite number was 3–ironic, isn't it, that she had three children.*

*Let me tell you about Pat's connection to God. Not only did she get phone calls from the archbishop and write letters to the seminarians–I found her phone number and address list–and what's inside? The Pope. Yes! I'm talking about former Pope John Paul's personal contact information in Vatican City. She is the only person I know who had the Pope's personal digits handy.*

## The Shepherdess

*Anyone who met Pat realized she had many childlike qualities. Innocence was one. I believe that is why she had a link to God. She was silly. Her laugh was contagious. She knew just how to raise your spirit if you needed a little pick-me-up. She was one of those rare, genuine people. If you asked her to do you a favor, you knew you could count on her. If she thought you could use a little help, whether you asked or not she was right there to lend a helping hand. She had that same loyalty to God. That's why He recruited her to be a part of His powerful team of earth angels. Everything she did on this earth was for God.*

*She always knew she had a "connection," so one day she asked God what her nickname should be. And this is why she said, "God has a sense of humor" because she heard a strong voice call her "Patty Cake".*

*Pat believed in signs. Every time she was looking for an answer or wanted some direction, she asked for a sign. One day she couldn't decide between buying an angel stature and paying $286 to fix a broken belt on her car. Both were the same price. So she asked for a sign. She prayed through the night and woke up to a strong voice saying, "Buy your Angel." She believed in that sign so much, she bought the angel. However, she still needed to fix her car. So she took her car back to the same shop, to the same mechanic. After going over the car once again, the mechanic told Pat he couldn't find anything wrong with her car!*

*Pat had a very creative mind and was known for using her artistic abilities. Instead of buying festive wreaths for every season, she would make them. Instead of buying greeting cards–you guessed it–she'd make her own. Each had a personal touch, of course. And this is how personal they were. As I thumbed one day through her St. Mary's church directory with photos of every family, I spied holes where the heads should be. Sometimes entire families were cut out. It wasn't that Pat didn't like them - just the opposite. She would cut out the photos to make people cards with their own pictures on it. Pat confided to me. She loved to put silly sayings next to their mouths to make them feel special.*

*Pat was famous for her answering machine message. At the message's end she would always say, "Have a Spirit-Filled Day" to remind us to live each day with the Lord in our hearts. We know she lived by that saying while she was here. Now she's shining down and working through us to help everyone "Have a Spirit-Filled Day!"*

*Pat loved to joke around, especially with our sister Mary Beth, who has also peacefully passed on. As they bonded together during motherhood, they grew to like Sesame Street. They liked one act so much that they started to act it out—voices and all. That act is "Bert and Ernie." The taller Pat played Bert, and loved to set up the jokes. The shorter Mary Beth was Ernie because she was always the sidekick, and pretty good at being the wise guy. Call them Bert and Ernie or call them Double Trouble, we know that tag team is together at last, celebrating their sisterhood, once again.*

## The Shepherdess

*During Pat's final weeks, a friend came by with a special pillow. The friend was Lutheran, so Pat started calling the gift "the non-denominational pillow" because she always accepted everyone, no matter of which religion. It became a family joke that created lots of laughs. When Pat did finally go to heaven, Kate and I bathed and dressed her. Being the dental hygienist she is, Kate starting cleaning out her mouth, which was drooping. So Kate said to Pat, "Here, have the non-denominational pillow–that'll cheer you up." Kate and I started laughing hysterically. The next thing we realized, Pat's once-drooping mouth was smiling, and that's how she left this world, with a smile on her face.*

*Pat always spoke about her "talks" with God, always talked openly about the pact she made with the Lord after she was diagnosed with breast cancer in 1996. Pat pleaded with God that she would live to see Christopher's 21$^{st}$ birthday. Her perseverance persisted and she lived two days beyond.*

*If you knew anything about Pat's driving, she was always running late. So, of course, we called her our little 'Speed Demon'. But the Elm Grove Police didn't find our Speed Demon's driving habits so funny. When they wrote her a ticket, they didn't have to ask for her license and registration. They knew it by heart–that's how many tickets she's had to pay. This was one thing Pat didn't think was very funny. In fact, she always wanted to 'get back' at the Elm Grove traffic officers. On her dying day, she got her wish. As she was being taken away in the hearse, we asked the driver to floor it. He did–and he took her on a joyride through the street of Elm Grove. This time she floored it all the way to heaven.*

On a rainy, spring day, Pat was buried in St. Mary's Cemetery in Elm Grove. Although the weather was overcast and cloudy, Patricia who was already born to eternal light, never shone so bright. Her prayer card offered her final prayer:

"Lord Jesus,
I give you my heart for it is yours
I give you my soul for you are mine
Take my hands that they may used
For Your greater honor and glory Lord
Now and forever!
Amen"

*My Prayer*
*Pat*

Recently I asked Mom to share her thoughts about breast cancer and its effect on the family. "Oh, it was a very trying time. You just never know how it started exactly," she replied. "Sometimes I'd feel a little guilty, wondering if it was something I did or didn't do–maybe taking extra vitamins or providing the children with some proper vitamins or minerals. Except for this cancer, no other major health issues were prevalent in the family. I look at it this way, the dear Lord freely gave me these children and He's free to take them back whenever He sees fit."

"Mary Beth was my elbowroom. Whenever I needed to

## The Shepherdess

talk, I would just head for her house, since it was so close. She was always busy but would say, 'Mom, let's sit down with a cup of coffee.' She was very different, laid back."

"As far as Pat goes, that girl couldn't do enough for me. She was a dear, dear daughter. If you went through our house more than 75% of my pictures, statues and clothes were from Pat. She just wanted to do–do–do for me whatever she could. At the end it was so beautiful. I would take her Communion each morning and we would sit and talk. There were no regrets. There is nothing worse than living with regrets, and I don't have any, thanks to God. Both girls died beautiful deaths. They are now both singing and glorifying God."

# Claire Marie

*Claire, the seventh-oldest, was born on October 15, 1960. Claire was named after a favorite nun whom Dorothy had read about. In the summer of 1975, Claire visited Terry and me when we were living in Portland, Oregon. As a special surprise, we drove her to Disneyland for a few days. On the way back, we stopped at the famous Sequoia Forest in California. Here Claire learned to drive a stick-shift car. At age fifteen she proudly drove through the huge, carved-out redwood.*

## St. Clare of Assisi

God of mercy, You inspired St. Clare with the love of poverty. By the help of her prayers, may we follow Christ in poverty of spirit and come to the joyful vision of your glory in the kingdom of heaven. We ask this through our Lord Jesus Christ, Your Son, Who lives and reigns with You and the Holy Spirit one God, forever and ever. Amen.

It seems apparent that, when individuals have life-threatening illnesses, faith plays a major part in the healing. The disciples established a ritual of praying for the sick to heal them. James 5:13-16 offers the following advice:

"Is any of you in trouble? He should pray. Is anyone happy? Let him sing songs of praise. Is any one of you sick? He should call the elders of the church to pray over him and anoint him with oil in the name of the Lord. And the prayer offered in faith will make the sick person well;

## The Shepherdess

the Lord will raise him up. If he has sinned, he will be forgiven. Therefore confess your sins to each other and pray for each other so that you may be healed. The prayer of a righteous man is powerful and effective."

Visions and apparitions have long been a vital part of religion. In the 1850's, St. Bernadette, a peasant girl, claimed to see the Virgin Mary a number of times at a grotto at Lourdes, in southwest France. While she became the object of criticism, today millions each year visit Lourdes as a Roman Catholic shrine. They make their pilgrimages drawn in the hope that they, too, will experience miraculous cures attributed to the shrine's waters.

In the cases of Mary Beth and Pat, an abiding faith provided an overwhelming sense of peace at the end of their lives. Along with the onset of cancer in the family came a greater awareness and closer connection to God, the Blessed Mother and especially the angelic realm. The highest form of communication we can have is with our Creator. Mary Beth prayed to the Lord and she readily told anyone who would listen, that she saw and was comforted by Raphael, the archangel of healing. In her time of need, Pat was in communion with God and prayerfully received messages from both the Lord and the Blessed Mother. She prayed and spoke to them as "best friends". As a result, she was given insight and a better understanding of her intended path coupled with a sense of love and peace. Likewise, Terry, a survivor, through meditation and prayer journaling feels closer to the Lord and His angelic team of helpers and believes that we all can call upon God and the angels for help and guidance. In prayer and silence, answers are received, and available for each of us to act upon.

Truly, angels *are* among us. A recent survey found that 55% of American adults (including one in five of those who say they have no religion) believe they have been protected by a guardian angel. Sociologist Christopher Bader of Baylor University, who conducted the survey, was surprised by the high number. Although not referring to guardian angels specifically, the Bible offers many instances of the doings of angels as protectors and guides. Psalms 91:1-12 states, "For he will command his angels concerning you to guard you in all your ways; they will lift you up in their hands, so that you will not strike your foot against a stone." We must put our complete faith in the Lord, yes, but if his angel army is assisting Him with assigned tasks, then we must recognize and appreciate their assistance as well.

In communicating with the Lord, one essential factor is silence. Psalms 46:10 tells us, "Be still, and know that I am God." Through meditation we find the awareness needed to communicate. Mom has always been able to reach this personal level with God. She meditates each morning, a ritual she has passed on to her children. Mary and Pat acquired this ability. Terry also, has received insight and a greater understanding of God and his angels through silent meditation. The following are excerpts of Terry's insights from prayer journaling:

In regard to committing to the Lord:

## The Shepherdess

"Who is God, you may ask? He is your loving Father and He sees you and knows you very well. Learn to know the Lord. He is a loving Father. Spend some quiet time and ask Him to help you get to know Him better. He is your best friend and can help you do anything and accomplish much in this world. Know that you are wrapped in His love and will help to unfold God's plan for you. Believe that it is happening as it truly is. Think and create positive thoughts.

Spiritual growth means remembering who you are and why you are on earth. Know and believe and it shall come to pass. You will find Me in the least likely of places. The answer is everywhere and is in everything. I am with you in all things and in all situations. We are one and cannot be separated. The only separateness is the one that you impose upon yourself by distractions away from Me. Keep centered, meditate, and pray often for guidance. I am the answer from within. Know and believe. It is not a mystery–it is the truth. It is Me in my purest form. Know the truth and speak the truth and you will have everlasting life. There is no other kind of life. You cannot have life without this. Drink of my blood and eat of my flesh and partake in communion with me always. We are one. Know this and you will not lose your way. Let peace and harmony prevail. Peace is the eternal knowing that all is right in my kingdom. Peace will allow the manifestation of all things. Go within and meditate. Feel Me and know Me from within, and all things will be revealed to you in time. I am the loving Father. Come to know Me better. If you fear Me as a father figure, think of Me as a mother figure. I am genderless. Your perception of Me will not alter what I am, which is what you are. We are love incarnate. We are one. This is my central concept of love and unity. Have you not heard of the saying there is strength in numbers? Well, we are all one. Imagine the strength that I can provide each of you and therefore to each other. Remember, where two or more are gathered in prayer, I am there."

<u>Releasing yourself to the Lord and establishing trust</u>:

"Listen and you will hear with open ears and see with open eyes, for the glory of God is around you. It surrounds you and will fill you with joy, if you but soak it in. Bathe in the warmth and love of the Creator. He will show you the way. We are around you to help; call on us and receive our help. It is there for the taking. Take our hand and follow the footsteps, for you are on the path to God our Father. Rest assured that your needs have been cared for and you will not want for anything. Trust and believe. Know that we love you and will be here for you. We know your thoughts and we love giving you help and direction. Believe and trust. HAVE A LEAP OF FAITH. Fast forward and see, envision and imagine and you will create your reality. We will be with you. Take our hands and we will walk together as you increase in spirituality. Pray, meditate and focus. We love you little one. Keep listening and you will hear. Knock and it will be opened, seek and you shall find. Remember all things are possible to those who believe and trust. Miracles happen every day. We will create your miracles with your

## The Shepherdess

help and trust in us – don't worry. You must totally release yourself by letting go your tension – breathe in the gift of the Holy Spirit. You are like a bird – you need to be free. Find freedom within and you will be at peace. Do not be afraid. Trust in God and He, in all His goodness, will provide for your needs. You will know God when you are at peace and let go of the burdens, for everything is cared for. Know and believe it is so. Breathe in the breath of salvation and release the fears that bind. They bind you to the earthly things which can easily be taken care of. But it is the soul that is everlasting and needs constant care and nourishment. Refresh your souls and your bodies and burdens will be refreshed and lifted.

Let Me be your strength and commit yourself to my work and Me. Feel my love and be at peace. Release the tensions and strains as they serve no purpose, but to restrict you and your need to be free. Free to soak up the energies of the universe that want to give to you abundantly. Look at the birds – they always have enough food. Look at the trees of the forest and the lakes of the stream; they are all of my Father's creations for your wonder and joy. Drink in the beauty of nature. Meditate and manifest your oneness with nature and you will know God, our Father. You will find the peace that was meant to be for you and those around you."

<u>Receiving and living with God's abundance for you</u>:
"Think fruitful thoughts. They will create peace and harmony, blessed with the grace of happiness. Be open to

the gifts of God's universe. Work for God's highest good to fulfill the mission of a soldier in His army. All limiting thoughts will be replaced with loving thoughts of charity. As it is often written in scripture, "I am and "We are one." The answers are clear. There is no such thing as privation if you believe. God is abundance, not want of any kind. Know this and it shall be so. Know who He is and feel His power within you to do His will every moment. Each act of Godliness will be acknowledged by God. What is His wish? Be clear about it and repeat what you already know to be true. He is abundance and He lacks nothing. Believe this–it is true. He will never fail you. Your only limitation is your limitation of your self's desires and manifestations. Be clear about what you wish to be and then reaffirm it. Angels are His messengers of love to you. Feel their presence and know that they are helping you as you have requested. Oh ye of little faith, like Thomas you are filled with doubt, but we know the goodness of your soul and your motivations are honorable if not human. Let go of your doubt and believe. Accept God's word and it will be yours. Believe in the Lord and His gifts will come to pass. God's universe is vast and abundant. Drink of His abundance as He bestows it on you. Meditate and pray, for the time is now. Know this and you will be saved.

We are around you and filling you with our love. Feel our presence and know that we are with you and will not abandon you. You are our child and we can never let you down. Remember, do not limit yourself and you will not be

## The Shepherdess

limited. Opportunities abound around you. Open your eyes and see them and make them flourish. Know that they were sent to you from our Father in heaven who loves you dearly. Remember to trust and believe. Flowers of abundance surround you. We will open the doors; you must walk through them joyfully and without reservation. Take God's hand and ours and we will walk with you on your journey. Be not afraid. It is by your salvation that you are redeemed and able to live a life of fulfillment."

These inspiring messages demonstrate just how available and willing the Lord is in meeting our every need. As the renowned French Jesuit and philosopher Teilhard de Chardin (1881-1955) stated, "We are not human beings having a spiritual experience. We are spiritual beings having a human experience." Our deeper being is of spirit and of knowing and understanding our connection to God and all things of nature. We must never be afraid to discuss our problems with God, and meditation is an ideal vehicle. Through meditation we can join forces with God and come to know and better understand the Lord. Our job is to serve others. In communion with God, we each come to learn our unique path of service.

As God is our loving Father, we must keep the communication channels open. We must talk to God and share what is on our minds and troubling our hearts, give our worries over to God to resolve. Then we must let go and focus again on doing service to others, as God takes care of our problems in ways we never could dream of.

Revelations 3:20 affirms how Jesus is ready and waiting, "Here I am! I stand at the door and knock. If anyone hears my voice and opens the door, I will come in and eat with him, and he with me."

Yes, we all have our moments of doubt. Even the saintly Mother Teresa admitted to such on occasion. With our faith and trust we can overcome these moments, turn them into powerful novenas that proclaim not only our desires but our belief in their plausibility. The "law of attraction" involves images and thoughts we hold in our minds. We must align our thoughts with our desires, be grateful and express our gratitude for all that we already have. It is difficult to bring more into our lives if we are ungrateful. Negative thoughts yield negative results. We should ask the Lord, and we shall receive. We should just believe and hold the end result of what we desire in our minds and let God take care of the details. When we emit clear, *exact* thoughts of what we desire, the relevant people, circumstances, and events line up in our lives. A case in point: Mom had an overwhelming desire to find a home for her family, a place where her children would be happy and have a fruitful family life. Mom had no idea what God's answer would be, but she stayed the course and allowed God's will to be done.

Again, *we should go back to our faith and belief in God.* We should envision the results we wish to achieve with exact mental images. What the mind can conceive and believe it can also achieve. The famous Indian physician Patanjali spoke this truth more than two thousand years

## The Shepherdess

ago. "When you are inspired by some great purpose, some extraordinary project, all your thoughts break their bonds. Your mind transcends limitations, your consciousness expands in every direction, and you find yourself in a new, great, and wonderful world," he put it. "Dormant forces, faculties and talents become alive, and you discover yourself to be a greater person by far than you ever dreamed yourself to be."

This belief unlocks God's loving force in the universe and lends us a sense of power that lets us not only own our desires but become part of their creation. If we believe that we are perfectly aligned in the universe to receive our desires, we *can*; this belief is the groundwork that produces the divine timing we desire. Keeping the faith through good times as well as bad times is the key to breeding this intent and its results.

Time and again it has been shown that if a person changes the way he views a situation, the situation itself will change. If we look at a situation negatively, guess what we find? But take the same situation—even an adverse one–and look for the positive or good and we perceive hidden blessings. Is our glass half full or half empty? We must have faith and trust in the Lord and, most of all, believe in the greatest good for all concerned.

A boy was flying a kite one day when it vanished behind a cloud. A man happening by asked the boy what he was doing holding the line. He told the man he was flying his kite. "But I don't see one," said the man. A tug by the boy soon brought the kite back into view. Sometimes our faith needs a tug and reminder that God is still there with our best interests at heart. Even in adverse times we must maintain a strong and unwavering faith.

Things *do* happen for a reason. The difficulty comes when we forget that most often God's plan differs from ours. If we look for signs to lead us and *believe* that God's will is being done we can reach reassurance and peace of mind.

Recently, I asked Mom if she believed in randomness or if events happen for a reason. Her reply was telling. "Things definitely happen for a reason," she said. "It's like running into someone that you haven't seen in over ten years. You must have some kind of unfinished business with them. I will give you a recent example. It was so weird. Yesterday I was at Kopps for an ice cream and I bumped into Margaret, a young girl who used to belong to our church. She had married and moved away. For a wedding gift, I had given her a goat, (Through Food for the Poor, a charitable organization, one can purchase and donate an animal to feed a Third World family). I had donated a goat in Margaret and her husband's name as my gift to them. She had thanked me a year ago, and had told me she was very touched by the gift, but was curious how I knew that her family used to raise goats? I told her that I had no idea. It had simply felt like the right gift for her. She had been so excited! Well, when I ran into her that day, I had not seen her for quite a while. Now she lives on the east side and is

## The Shepherdess

prominent in the Neumann Center at UW–M. She used to come to our church when she was single and she reminded me so much of our dear Mary Beth. She even looked like Mary, acted like her, and had long, straight hair as well. She was a Mary Beth duplicate. She had stopped by church one time during the year to show me her wedding pictures, but that had been a long time ago. When I saw her she ran up and hugged me. It was so neat. She told me that she was going to come back to OLGH just to see me. What she said next almost floored me. She was getting custard to take to the Seminarians. I said, 'Oh my God, the Seminarians are a mission of mine, truly dear to my heart. This mission was my daughter Pat's as well. Before Pat died, she asked, 'Mom–please keep this mission going? We need prayers to have more men enter the priesthood." To this, Margaret replied, "You know, two friends of mine are currently in the seminary, and I'm taking them a treat and fervently pray for them each day." I was so pleased! It was such an amazing moment. A Mary look-alike undertaking Pat's most important mission!"

No, there is no such thing as coincidence. Things *do* happen for a reason. The principle of synchronicity comes to mind. Swiss psychiatrist Carl Jung, a colleague of Freud, is deemed the discoverer of this principle. A non-causal dynamic links events having a similar meaning by their coincidence in time rather than sequentially. In other words, there is no simple cause and effect as we know it. We must take this to heart, be positive, and keep our minds open to the "meaningful coincidences" that may present themselves every day.

We can start with an understanding of our Father in Heaven. We are all His children. We each have the ability to learn to know God and join in communion with Him. He speaks to each of us differently, clearly wants to have a unique and personal experience with each of us. Some of us find God through organized religion, others of us outside the bounds of the conventional church. But both ways can be equally spiritual.

Mom is a living example of this. Her deep spiritual connection to God comes through the Catholic Church, yes, but also through means outside of formal religion. If we look up the word Catholic, we find two Greek meanings and pronunciations. 'Catholic' pertains to the Roman Catholic Church; and 'Catholic' means "universal." While Mom's devotion to the Catholic Church is exceptional, at the same time she opens her arms and her heart universally to anyone and everyone, regardless of ethnicity, faith, or position.

# Carolyn

*Carolyn was the eighth-oldest, born March 28, 1962. She was named after Princess Carolyn of Monaco, Grace Kelley's daughter. If you ever played a sport and winning was important, you would pick Carol to be on your team. Growing up, she was always a top pick, ahead of even most of the boys. I especially enjoyed playing softball and tennis with Carol.*

**A Prayer of Healing through Worship**

Heavenly Father, We come into Your presence to love and adore You. Thank You for Your love and Your desire for union with us. We welcome all that You wish to do through this healing prayer. We open ourselves to communication with You and Jesus through the ministry of the Holy Spirit. Come Holy Spirit, anoint us with healing so deep it reaches back into our blood line; with healing so wide it impacts our friends and relatives; with healing so high it draws us into Your holiness. Holy Spirit, come with Your fire. Our Father Which Art In Heaven–

Almost twelve years ago our daughter Nicole met a young man named Rick, a cousin of Nicole's best high-school friend. Nicole had moved from Wisconsin to Arizona, but, as we know, everything happens for a reason. Destiny, transcending time and space barriers, found them. Rick grew up in Shawano, Wisconsin, and his family had a home on the lake. He had played sports growing up, a perfect fit for Nicole. After years of long-

## The Shepherdess

range dating and both in jobs in different cities and states, they were both able to find a common place to call home. We were pleased when they decided to move to Scottsdale. Rick was a business major from Arizona State University. Nicole had graduated from Northern Arizona University in broadcast journalism. On February 12, 2006, they were engaged, the wedding planned for September 2, 2006. Considering that more than 90% of the family and guests lived in Wisconsin and Illinois, they decided to marry in Wisconsin. The wedding prompted great anticipation, amid months of planning. The Wedding Mass would be held at St. Robert Catholic Church in Shorewood and the reception at the Milwaukee Art Museum. By late summer excitement was building, amid frequent trips to Milwaukee to finalize the plans for the event.

However, since early summer Dad's health had been deteriorating. He had been in and out of the hospital, with impaired circulation in his lower legs. The doctors proposed amputation as one remedy, but with no guarantees. The surgery itself was a major risk. There was high probability that a clot could dislodge, resulting in a massive stroke or death. After weighing this, the family ruled out surgery. In July, Dad entered a nursing home. Several times after, amid deteriorating health, he was admitted to St. Mary's Hospital. Re-stabilized, he went back to the nursing home in August. Hopes were that he would regain his strength and return home.

The weekend before the wedding, Terry and Nicole

had flown to Milwaukee to finalize last-minute plans. In between, they managed to stop in and visit Dad and share the details of the wedding with him. On Sunday when they left his room, he smiled and motioned goodbye with his hand in his cute, unique manner. They were happy. They would see him again in only a few days.

Early Tuesday morning, August 29, 2006–Mother of Perpetual Help day–Christine and Mom visited Dad. As part of her recent daily routine, Mom brought him Communion. The nurse pulled Mom aside and told her that Dad had taken a turn for the worst. He was not expected to live through the day. Soon all the children congregated in the nursing home. The Bergs arrived as well. Before the crowd filled the room, Mom asked Dad if he was afraid to die. Dad shook his head, smiled, and replied, "No." This brought great peace to her heart. The family entered and prayed together. Father Charlie came and administered the Sacrament of the Sick. Late that morning Dad looked up toward the ceiling and motioned. Maybe, just maybe, Mary Beth and Pat were there to accompany him on his transition? Shortly after, surrounded by his loving family, he passed away.

The funeral was planned for a week later, so as not to conflict with the wedding plans. Always thinking of others, Mom did not want to detract from Nicole and Rick's joy. But, after a lengthy discussion, most of the family agreed it would be better to have the funeral first, and then move into a blissful occasion. Dad's wake and funeral were

## The Shepherdess

rescheduled for Thursday, two days later. Everyone was fine with the outcome.

Needless to say, it was a bittersweet week. With only a couple days to do so, Carol and Kate both worked hard to help Mom with all the preparations. On Thursday, August 31, Dad's wake and funeral took place at Our Lady of Good Hope. The church was filled with family, friends, work colleagues, and his fellow Legionnaires. Meanwhile, Mom exhibited a rare strength and resolve. She was amazingly resilient. Her demeanor was saintly as she greeted each mourner with open arms. She has a way of speaking that sometimes seems to come directly from God. That day she worked to comfort all who attended, to convince them of what she fully accepted–that Erv was in a far better place with God. As I watched, I couldn't help but notice that each person to whom she spoke heeded her words with great interest and feeling. It was like the old, famous E.F. Hutton commercial. When Dorothy spoke, people listened. Instinctively sensing Mom's deep and spiritual connection to the Lord, people seemed to pay attention. Even in her deepest tragedy, Dorothy was concerned far more about others than herself.

The service was beautiful and moving–a celebration of the life of a wonderful man who had loved his family deeply and had devoted much of his time to others. On the airplane coming back to Wisconsin, Nicole, Terry, and I had written the eulogy, which Terry, once again, was chosen to deliver. It went as follows:

# Birk

*Dad*

*Like Mother always says... "Everything good happens on a Tuesday. That's why we all know the dear Lord had a plan when He took this husband, father of eleven and grandfather of thirty-one to heaven.*

*Let me tell you about our Dad.... Better known as 'The Big E.' I can tell you... he had one of the strongest work ethics I know. He worked day and night to provide for this family of thirteen... and with nine girls... there were certainly a lot of wants... 'I want this... I want that!'... We may not have gotten everything we wanted but we certainly got everything we needed... and more. I think we can all say we respect the value of a dollar and have a true appreciation for giving to the less fortunate after living in that household.*

*Speaking of that house, some of you may remember... when we moved from Milwaukee's inner city to what our mom called, "the most beautiful house in Milwaukee!".... And it STILL is! You may not know it... but our parents prayed long and hard to find the perfect house to raise this large family comfortably. Of course, a prerequisite was that the house had to be within walking distance of a Catholic Church. They finally found the house on August 15–the Feast of the Assumption. But Dad wouldn't move into the house until it passed inspection... his inspection! Talk about 'sweat equity'! Since eight children had lived in the house before our family, there were a lot of nicks and scratches on the walls... And it just wasn't good enough for*

## The Shepherdess

his family to move into. So every night, after working all day at Perlick's he would stop by the house... and paint and fix up... every room... one at a time. As some of you shared, he also did this at some of my brothers and sisters houses too. And since he was the 'Commander in Chief,' he would park HIS car in the garage while yours would sit on the driveway. He put his paint brushes in the refrigerator and blasted his WEZW music by the hour and you had to be at his beck and call.

Back to our house... we finally moved in right before Christmas in December of 1968... OH... WHAT a Christmas it WAS! Our whole family went to Midnight Mass that Christmas Eve... the first official Mass at Our Lady of Good Hope. Little did we know... each and every one of us would get married here and Dad would always drive us girls to the church in the BIG RED WAGON on OUR BIG DAY!

Dad was always a devoted member of the church... from Friday night fish fries to serving on many committees. And we can't forget about all the festivals. He was always there to lend a helping hand because the members of the church were always like a second family to my parents.

Now we all have a lot of funny stories as kids but I think we can all remember our fabulous family outings. We couldn't leave the house without looking like the Von Trapp family in our matching outfits, and a buddy. And remember "Twosies"? Dad would always say, "Everyone get in the car and he would tell us to "Count the noses!" a task that sometimes got delegated.... Perhaps that's why Paul was left at Muskego Beach.

Dad may have been a quiet, personal man... but he had a special way with KIDS... especially his dozens of grandchildren. One day Ashley was at Mom and Dad's house and GRANDPA was babysitting. He took her by the hand and took her down to the basement for the first time ever. However, this was a crowded basement. After winding through the messy maze, all of a sudden he stopped and there at their feet were Disney movies. She got to pick any one she wanted... to watch that day. As for the Weber family, Grandpa and Grandma would take them every year to the State Fair for a day of special treats on them. When the kids would ask, "Can I have that? .... Grandpa would always respond... TELL THE LADY!"

All of us know, when you went to our parents' house, you would always find the BIG E in his favorite recliner with his FEET propped up... listening to or watching old sit-coms like " I Love Lucy" or any sporting event. Sports were his passion. He just had to be in what he referred to as 'The Best Seat in the House'! The love of sports is probably why Margaret couldn't find Dad for a very important moment at her wedding... The Bridal Dance. After searching the entire Mequon Country Club, she found him in the Members-Only Room, watching baseball. Margaret said to Dad, 'Let's go... you have to dance with Mom as part of the Bridal Dance.' Dad calmly replied with one of his classic responses, 'FINK ME... it's game four of the World Series.... I'll be there in a

## The Shepherdess

*minute.'*

Dad was also a man who liked good food. Dorothy's kitchen was always a hot spot, but on a rare occasion he would treat the family to a Sunday night out at Ponderosa. And Dad would always say, 'We're going to Pondy's and you can have ANYTHING you want.' He also went through phases with his other favorite restaurants... Remember George Webb, Baker's Square, Wren's for a fish fry and who can forget midnight runs for Albanese's pizza? And for dessert, you could always find him at home in his den. With a popcorn tin filled with enough candy to satisfy any sweet tooth.

On Saturdays he always had the family car washed. He cut the grass and by the afternoon his car usually FOUND ITS WAY to the Kmart parking lot. He always loved shopping for gadgets and little treasures especially if they were on a BLUE LIGHT SPECIAL. This Kmart fascination is probably one of the biggest contributing factors to the current state of our parents' basement!

Our dad was a patriot. He loved our country as much as he loved our family and God. That's whey he always honored Memorial Day and celebrated the 4$^{th}$ of July by parading with his fellow Legionnaires from the Gold Star Post 505. If you didn't know, our dad is a Korean War veteran. He served in the Marine Corps as a medic stationed in Japan for several years before our parents were married.

Our parents were married on October 6, 1951 and it

would have been *fifty-five years this October. Our Dad loved our mom so much and he would always do special things for her. He brought home her favorite set of China from Japan along with a string of cultured pearls he gave her on their wedding day. It is especially an honor for me to see my daughter, Nicole walk down the aisle wearing those pearls this Saturday. The necklace along with all of the love that comes with it, is promised to be passed down for so many generations to come.*

*Dad is the patriarch... The foundation of this family and, since he is the decision-maker, I asked him when he was sick in the hospital, 'What would you like to see happen?" I was referring to options for his care. He looked me straight in the eye and said... 'Whatever is the will of God!'*

*On Tuesday (remember, Mother always said that Everything Good Always Happens on a Tuesday... Mom gave Dad Holy Communion for the last time. Shortly after, he sat up in bed, raised both of his arms straight up to the sky, and looked to the heavens. His eyes were wide... filled with awe and wonder! Then he reverently made the sign of the cross. He lay back down and looked side to side and closed his eyes. My personal belief is when he looked from side to side... he saw his two beautiful angelic daughters—Mary Beth and Pat.*

*With almost his entire family at his bedside, he left this earth to go back home to meet our Creator.*

*We thank you Dad for being the Father you were,*

## The Shepherdess

*and we know you are at peace. Enjoy your well-deserved eternity... in the Heavenly Kingdom!*
*We love you, Dad.*

Everyone has the opportunity for salvation through faith. "Where, O death, is your victory? Where, O death, is your sting? The sting of death is sin, and the power of sin is the law," reads 1 Corinthians 15:55-58. "But thanks be to God! He gives us the victory through our Lord Jesus Christ. Therefore, my dear brothers, stand firm. Let nothing move you. Always give yourself fully to the work of the Lord, because you know that your labor in the Lord is not in vain." Yes, Dad is in a better place where love abounds and peace is eternal. Dad's sons and sons-in-law were honored as his pallbearers, and he was buried at Holy Cross cemetery, in St. Therese Chapel.

A few months later I asked Mom how she was coping. She responded, "After Dad passed away, I adopted Jesus as my *best friend*. I can honestly say He has been walking with me every moment of the day. All fear has been taken away from me regarding living alone, which I thought I could never do." Everyone has moments in life where we feel we are all alone and isolated. Just as in the story of Jesus, 'Footprints in the Sand,' we come to realize that at these times in our lives the Lord is truly carrying us. God is always there for us unconditionally. In her time of need, Mom instinctly knew to reach out to the Lord. She knew they would be spending considerably more time together.

Last year I asked Mom how she can continue to accept

God's will and live her life in a consistently positive manner. Was it simply plain faith? She replied, "Yes, that's certainly what it is. You've said it in a nutshell. 'God's ways are not our ways, if we truly love Jesus, we will accept simply that "God's Will" is done.' He wants it that way. His ways are not the ways *we* intended it to be. No, they aren't, and sometimes you don't even want it to happen that way. Sometimes it ends up even much, much better. You just bow to the exceptional ways of the Lord. He is all knowing. Most of the time I am not so smart, but the dear Lord gave me common sense and lots of it. From this common sense I have realized that we can't do things on our own, we must rely on the Lord."

Now Mary Beth, Pat and Dad had made their transitions to heaven. Amazingly, each had died in peace, their passings freely accepted. Mom elaborated, "Oh, yes, they were all resigned. It was very sad and all, but it seemed like it was meant to be. Prayer wins all. We all prayed so fervently, 'Lord, if it is your will, please spare Erv and these young girls. But it is not *my* will but *Thy* will that will be done.' We just prayed and prayed and prayed our hearts out with them and for them day after day."

The week was an emotional roller-coaster. Wedding preparations, Dad's death and funeral, and then came Friday, September 1. The wedding rehearsal was held at St. Robert's, followed by the rehearsal dinner party, the kickoff for the celebration weekend. Festive, personal, and elegant seemed to define the theme. The ever-thoughtful

## The Shepherdess

Rick and Nicole planned a several-hour voyage on the *Edelweiss 1*, a private charter boat. Stepping aboard in downtown Milwaukee for the Rehearsal Festivities, each guest received a "boarding pass." Once everyone was accounted for, the *Edelweiss* left for a leisurely cruise up the Milwaukee River and out into Lake Michigan for a glimpse of the Milwaukee Art Museum, the venue for the wedding reception. Rick's dad, Fred, entertained everyone with his music, and Terry and I toasted the soon-to-be-newlyweds with a poem. Becky entertained with a musical dance routine. The food was scrumptious, the party boat rocking. From the minute Nicole and Rick handed everyone their boarding passes until the final docking, everyone had a wonderful, memorable time. Unfortunately, Mom was too tired to attend. She wanted to conserve her energy for the wedding festivites. She was truly missed!

The wedding took place on a sunny, late summer perfect day. St. Robert's was nobly beautiful with its abundant stained-glass windows. I'll never forget the anticipation as Terry and I stood outside with Nicole in her last moments as a single woman. Then the cues came and Terry, Nicole's matron of honor, made her entrance. That left just one more entrance–Nicole's. Terry had vanished behind the closed church doors. We waited patiently. Then, to the sound of the Milwaukee Symphony Orchestra, the doors drew open. I'll never forget that walk. So many thoughts flooded my mind. I remember thinking, "How could Erv have done this *nine times?*" It was so emotionally exhausting. Giving my daughter Nicole away was very difficult, but knowing that Rick was there for the hand-off made it so much easier. Nicole and Rick had a special candle lit for Dad and one for Rick's grandfather, two special people who were there in spirit. Rick's Uncle Steve and my brother Tom performed the readings. Being the oldest granddaughter, Mom gave Nicole the prized pearls as her wedding shower gift. Dad had brought the pearls home from Japan some fifty-five years before, for his bride's wedding present. Nicole proudly wore the pearls on her wedding day.

    The reception at the Milwaukee Art Museum was nothing less than spectacular. The dinner was outstanding, with toasts from the heart. Several people commented that the sight of the lake from the dining area reminded them of a view from the *Titanic*. In my toast I emphasized to everyone that this was in fact the "Love Boat." My brother John entertained the guests by singing with the orchestra. A father-daughter ritual especially meaningful to Nicole and me was set to "Forever Young," a song that Nicole and I had danced to years earlier at her dance recital. Finally came the bridal dance, and it struck me. Nicole was now Mrs. Richard Beyer. They made such an elegant couple as they seemed to float across the floor.

    At the wedding Mom exhibited a resiliency no less than amazing. She talked to everyone. She even danced. Wanting to make sure Nicole had her special day, she somehow was able to suspend the sad events of only days before.

    In four short days the family had gone through

## The Shepherdess

an incredible journey. We had said goodbye to Dad, the patriarch, and had grieved. Then we celebrated a monumental event in spectacular fashion. Everyone saw and knew that Mom's unselfish attitude and willingness to trust and accept the Lord's will enabled Nicole to have her special day. By showing everyone "the way," Mom again led by example.

# Paul Gerard

*Paul, the ninth-oldest and second son, was born on May 9, 1963. Paul was named after St. Paul and St. Gerard. In 1979, when I was coaching grade-school basketball at Our Lady of Good Hope, Paul, age sixteen, assisted me one season. Our team had been struggling and had lost three close games in a row. Due to work conflicts, I was unable to attend the next game. Paul took over, and our team won by one point. I asked Paul if he could identify the difference. He said, "In a word, coaching!"*

## Prayer to St. Gerard for a Mother with Child

O almighty and everlasting God, through the Holy Spirit, you prepared the body and soul of the glorious Virgin Mary to be a worthy dwelling place of your divine Son. Through the same Holy Spirit, you sanctified St. John the Baptist, while still in his mother's womb. Hear the prayers of your humble servant who implores you, through the intercession of St. Gerard, to protect me amid the dangers of childbearing and to watch over the child with which you blessed me. May this child be cleansed by the saving water of baptism and, after a Christian life on earth, may we, both mother and child, attain everlasting bliss in heaven. Amen.

For Christmas of 2006, Mom announced she had everything she needed in life and wanted no Christmas presents whatsoever. If people chose to, they could donate to a cause she felt strongly about—purchasing a house for a poor family in Guatemala, at a cost of $2,600. Family and friends did not take mom's cause lightly. Seemingly everyone donated. Mom had prayed that she could secure the funds to make it happen. She knew first hand how much a home could make a difference in a family's life. Just as with her own family, her prayers were answered. Mom was able to turn over $3,500! Father David was so ecstatic that he made an announcement of this gift in his homily the following Sunday.

On March 30, 2007 Mom celebrated her eightieth birthday with a surprise luncheon at Mequon Country Club. Claire picked her up late in the morning. Mom thought she was going to see Tricia perform in a school play. Claire told Mom she had to make a quick stop at Mequon Country Club to pay a bill. As they both walked into the lobby, family and friends surprised her, and helped her celebrate the beginning of her ninth decade. Margaret composed a poem just for the occasion entitled "Cherished Mother." The poem made detailed mention of many deeds Mom had done for the family through the years. Her caring manner, wisdom, tenderness, heart of gold—these summed Mom's efforts through the years. Margaret ended by calling Mom the "Greatest Mother and Quilter"' of all–a title only Mom could claim.

For Easter of 2007 Mom sent us a beautiful cross made of a palm frond with a special note. "Every year this nice man at church makes crosses from palms and he gives me one. They are all different and quite beautiful. I never throw them away, but I have five and wanted to share one with you. Since its receipt, I keep the cross near my desk as a sign of the Lord's commitment and dedication to all of us." Even at age eighty, Mom still hungered to contribute to the community in any way she could. In September, 2007, she was chosen Honorary Chairperson for the Our Lady of Good Hope Parish Picnic. The parish bulletin provided the following:

Dorothy Wiencek – Honorary Chairperson

Dorothy Wiencek is this year's Honorary Chairperson. Dorothy, as wife and mother, continues to watch over her family following the death of her beloved husband. She is well known at OLGH and her tireless energy, sweet smile, gentleness in prayer before the Lord, and a friend to all. Yes, Dorothy watches over her OLGH family as well. She is a role model for us, a reminder of what it means to belong to "the family of God." Dorothy continues to be a positive presence in the life of our parish family.

The following week Mom extended an invitation to the parish picnic in the church bulletin. It read as follows:

The OLPH parish Picnic – Sunday, September 9, 2007

Invitation from the Honorary Chairperson

The Wiencek Family Picnics were the best! Now, I'm looking forward to my "Second Family" picnic. My friends at OLGH are the best! I will be praying for the success of this event.

~ Dorothy Wiencek

The parish picnic was, in fact, a great success. A fine

## The Shepherdess

band entertained, and there was a raffle. Mom's two quilts made for the occasion were received by two lucky winners. The parishioners enjoyed a day of fun, music, relaxation, good food, and fellowship.

In the fall of 2007 Mom and I decided to do a family project together. I had access to some green peridot heart-shaped gemstones. With Mom's encouragement, Terry and I designed a miniature plaque for each family. The inscription read "Bless Our Family–May this green Peridot heart serve as a reminder of the uniqueness of our family and the eternal promise of hope." Each plaque had a peridot heart to symbolize the heart projecting outward. We intended to surprise each family with one for Christmas, and hoped each would display it in the home as a sign of unity, hope and love.

When I purchased the gems, I immediately sent them to Mom in Milwaukee to have them blessed by a priest and bless them in her own manner. After two weeks the stones were returned to me with a note from Mom, "Dear Rick, Mission accomplished. Our dear Father Charlie said a beautiful prayer over these gemstones. I sprinkled some holy water on the stones as well. You are so kind to do something so special. Father Charlie would like to see the finished product." It was a great feeling of accomplishment mailing the packages to each family and to Father Charlie. We also sent Mom the same heart-shaped peridot made into a pendant for Christmas to token her role as family matriarch, and 'heart' of the family. This, I felt, would unify our family even more. Mom's support paid off, and all the families are displaying the plaques prominently in their homes.

For Christmas of 2008, Mom announced she had an idea. Her children responded, "Mom, please–not another house!" She laughed and said, "Any small gift will help the poor families." Again the Wienceks succeeded, spearheaded by Mom, and were able to send a check for $400 to Food for the Poor. "This donation provided one hundred chickens for numerous families, three piglets for one family, and one very-needed water pump for a thirsty village," Mom put it.

Much like a teacher, Mom plants the seeds of God's wisdom in the hearts and minds of those she touches. Colossians 3:15-17 gives the following advice, "Let the peace of Christ rule in your hearts, since as members of one body you were called to peace. And be thankful. Let the word of Christ dwell in you richly as you teach and admonish one another with all wisdom, and as you sing psalms, hymns and spiritual songs with gratitude in your hearts to God. And whatever you do, whether in work or deed, do it all in the name of the Lord Jesus, giving thanks to God the Father through him."

Leading by example, Mom continues to be a role model for her family and her community through her ongoing service and random acts of kindness. She has a rare understanding of the word "love," which by definition can mean any number of things, depending on context and figure of speech. Love can be a profoundly passionate

## The Shepherdess

feeling for another. Love can also be a feeling of warm personal attachment or deep affection, as for a parent, child, or friend. Yet another definition sees love as concern for the well-being of others—say, the love for a neighbor. The word L-O-V-E as an anagram can yield <u>Listen</u>, <u>Overlook</u>, <u>Verbalize</u>, and <u>Effort</u>, four powerful words that seem to describe the backbone of any loving relationship. Love should be the driving force or motivation behind helping others and thereby doing God's work. True to the first impression I had of her, Mom continues to do all with great purpose and passion. Without question her heart is filled with love. Her sole purpose is to love and serve the Lord by serving others. Her passion is–humanity. Home is a place the feet may leave but not the heart. Love is the master key to the gate of happiness. Through this gate she nourishes friends, neighbors–all God's creatures.

Moreover, because she lives in the now, Mom is happy, comfortable, and content with who she is as a person and what she subscribes to in terms of ethics, principals, and values. I asked Mom what she feels is the secret to a successful life. She replied, "You must keep a positive attitude and everything will fall into place the way you hope it to. Attitude is one of my favorite words, but a close second would be 'awareness.' You must be aware of your surroundings. Yes, attitude and awareness–two important words."

A priest well summed up the importance of attitude one day. He had recently been diagnosed with cancer. The doctor had told him he had less than two years to live. He told his congregation, "My dear people, if I live for two years, I get to be with you for that time. If I die, I get to be with God for eternity. If you have a better offer than that, take it! Live your life with love and purpose."

One concept that Mom has always lived by is forgiveness and moving forward. With thirteen people in such close quarters, disputes were bound to occur. Mom always urged and facilitated swift reconciliations. The ability to let go of anger leads to the path of healing. Asked how many times we should forgive, Jesus replied, "Seventy times seven." Moses started many of his messages with the word "Today." We need to reflect on today, not live in the past. Forgiving ourselves is as important as forgiving others. Reconciliation takes two or more people, but forgiveness takes only one. Consider this, when we enter heaven's gate someday, there is a good chance we may see people there whom we did not expect. Just possibly, some people have lower spiritual IQs. It's like a C student doing C work and an A student doing C work. Who has made the most out of their circumstances? We must be tolerant of others, refrain from judgment and accept people for who they are.

Furthermore, complaining about others can backfire. A man went for a checkup and told the doctor he was having an issue with his wife. She was going deaf, and it was becoming very irritating. The doctor advised the man to test his wife. He went home, stood forty feet from her, and asked, "Honey, what's for supper?" He then repeated the

## The Shepherdess

words at thirty, twenty, and then ten feet from her. Getting no response, he went up and whispered directly in her ear, "Honey, what's for Supper?" She turned to him and replied, "For the fifth time–chicken!"

Not too long ago, a priest related a story in a sermon. In his teens, the priest had purchased a ticket for an all-important pro hockey game. But the same night he had a date with a very pretty girl in his class, a date he had sought for a long time. He finally decided that he would give his ticket to a friend at his school and go on the date. At the hockey match there was a drawing. Because of his seat number, the boy won a new car. The priest told us that he never saw that girl–or that boy–again! He went on to another subject. Five minutes later he stopped and said, "Did I tell you that the car was a Mustang Convertible?" His remark got a laugh, but he was making a vital point. We all make decisions, both good and bad. We should just bless our decisions and live with them.

Confession is how God forgives our sins after baptism. We should acknowledge our sins with truth and honesty. Did not the Prodigal Son decide to return home? If we are truly sorry and confess our sins, God is a just God who forgives us. Mom and Dad regularly went to confession. The kids did as well, as part of their earlier education. "When it came to high school, the children were on their own, but usually went to confession at Christmas and Easter or for general reconciliation," Mom explained. "I encouraged them to attend, but did not put too much pressure on them. I wanted them to understand it and appreciate it. It's very healing to a person, and, when you leave, you leave a new human being."

This reminded me of another anecdote. A twelve-year old exited a confessional utterly distraught. She had received a penance of three "Hail Marys." With a look of despair she said to her mom, "But I only know one!"

Most of us are average, normal people living our lives the best we can. We obey the laws. We do the right and honest thing, and give praise to the Lord. Life's aim is not worldly fame, but doing as much as possible for others and for the greater honor and glory of God. Again Mom is grounded in the present, finding ways to serve others each day. Instead of daydreaming or pondering what to do, she propels herself into action.

At church and in meditation it is important to listen–really listen–to God's word. In trust and quiet lies our strength. Not listening may prevent divine timing. Psalms 46:10 tells us, "Be still, and know that I am God; I will be exalted among nations, I will be exalted on the earth." I once heard someone say that the basis of evil is the inability to sit still. We all must learn to 'quiet our minds' in order to be receptive to the word of God.

About a year ago someone pointed out that the letters in "Bible," God's written word, stand for, "Basic Instructions Before Leaving Earth." When I passed this on to Mom, she replied, "Wow, how interesting! If you really do think about it, that makes a great deal of sense."

## The Shepherdess

Mom does not spend considerable time reading the Bible, but she listens and reflects at daily Mass. She also enjoys reading Catholic books, magazines, and pamphlets. A few months ago she told me she had just read *Fatima, Through the Eyes of a Child*, a short book about Our Lady of Fatima appearing to three young children in a city in Portugal. Its message is wonderful and fit for all age groups, she said.

While Mom has long supported Capuchin Priests in general, the last few years she has turned her attention to helping those at the Solanus Casey Center in Detroit. Her prayers and quilts have been a great help to the ministry there. Last spring she sent another quilt to Father Daniel Fox, a quilt with a special sports theme. Once more touched by Mom's generous contribution, Father Daniel took the time to send her a special card featuring the Blessed Mother on the front. The card read, "Many thanks again for your beautiful quilt. I am grateful that you think of me and of our ministry here. I am sure God will bless you for your generosity. You have a great spirit. Thank you. Life goes on here. Our days seem warmer and sunnier. That's wonderful. What's more amazing to me is that you bring Sun and warmth the entire year just by being alive. Thank you. Love and Prayers, Father Dan." Equally appreciative of his response, Mom placed the card in a picture frame, and it now sits proudly in her living room.

The quilt was a wonderful gift, but short-lived. Not long after it arrived, there was a fire in a nearby home.

The family lost just about everything. Father felt called to donate the special quilt to the family with several boys who loved sports. Months later I had the opportunity to speak with Father Dan. He told me that Mom just continues to do the Lord's work, has truly mastered the "art of giving." Moreover, Father Dan told me it was incredible that I had decided to call him on that particular day. Only moments before had he finished writing an article for the Solanus Casey Center's monthly newsletter, an article featuring Mom. Under his column "Fox Trottings," he wrote the following,

"I have a wonderful friend named Dorothy in Wisconsin who makes us quilts for our fund-raising auctions. They are really beautiful. She has raised eleven children and the Lord knows she is used to hard work. Dorothy keeps herself busy quilting blankets in order to support our outreach and ministry here at the Solanus Casey Center! It isn't just the blankets that give warmth; but her generous heart and giving spirit warm my soul."

# Margaret Ann

*Margaret, the tenth child, was born on September 13, 1964. She was named after a special neighbor, Margaret Eis. Margaret, Terry's "non-identical twin," often babysat for our family. We would come home to find our refrigerator full of beautiful "artwork," a talent she passed on to her children. Her bread-making abilities are renowned to this day.*

## St. Margaret Mary Alacoque

May the offerings of Thy people be accepted by Thee, O Lord: and grant that we may be inflamed by that Divine fire which coming from the heart of Thy Son, burnt vehemently within blessed Margaret Mary. Through the same Our Lord, Jesus Christ, Thy Son, Who liveth and reigneth with Thee, in the unity of the Holy Ghost, one God, world without end. Amen.

Becoming part of the Wiencek family in 1973 gave me a very proud feeling. I had come from a Lutheran background and the Wiencek family was Catholic, but the difference in faith never was an issue. It was readily apparent that I was viewed and respected as a person, as one of God's many children. At the time, while my understanding of the Catholic faith was minimal, I could see so clearly that this religion was the backbone of this wonderful family. It was a beautiful religion, and I wanted to learn more. I had not attended church regularly for years before I had met Terry. I believed in God but felt that church-going would be on my time frame. I was a C & E (Christmas and Easter only) Lutheran.

Many God-fearing people do not attend church. In a January, 2008, *USA Today* article titled, "Many find God outside of church," a survey found that almost three-quarters of non-churchgoers believe that God exists. About just as many say churches are "full of hypocrites." Nearly 80% agree that modern Christianity "is more about organized religion than loving God and loving people." Slightly over half believed Jesus died and was resurrected. Non-churchgoers envision a more generic deity that accommodates every theocratic system, even those which contradict each other, says Ed Stetzer, the Director of Life Way Research.

Such informational statistics offer a glimpse into what a cross-section of our country believes. It is quite interesting that so many *non*-churchgoers believe in a supreme being, a conclusion that is strong only if one has an understanding of religion and has done some soul-searching. Possibly these people are in fact, religious folks like my family but simply choosing not to attend. As for the next point—some three-quarters of those surveyed saw the churches as "full of hypocrites"–I at times have felt the same. By definition a hypocrite is a person pretending to own virtues, morals, or religious principles that he does not actually possess, and his actions belie his appearances. Mom, for one, has *never* talked about other parishioners' attendance at church or lack thereof. She has taught us that the decision is a personal one, between a person and God. However, if a person doesn't attend church due to so-called hypocrites, isn't he hypocritical himself? A basic Christian ritual *is* that of attending church as a group. And doesn't pointing out a hypocrite mean passing judgment on others? "Judge not, lest you too be judged," advises Matthew 7:1. We all are sinners. Perhaps the "hypocrites" may have realized the error of their ways and attend church to ask God's forgiveness. Wouldn't it be better for everyone to come together to hear and share God's word as Jesus has taught us?

The fact that over half of non-churchgoers share the fundamental Christian belief that Jesus died and rose again is encouraging. To believe so, one must have an understanding of the great mystery of the Resurrection, which in itself shows a strong faith in life after death.

Many of those surveyed have a concern with the church organization itself, and have difficulty understanding how the church can instill in us that we should love one another. The response and challenge to these people is simple. Don't turn your back. Attend church. Make a difference. Be a change agent! The church is not the building but the congregation. We must remember Jesus' message to all. Where two or more gather in his name, He is present.

Lastly, non-churchgoers have a generic image of God. There are many fine religions in the world. A generic view, in a way, grants credibility and thereby acceptance to not one but many. Romans 10:12-13, for example, tells us,

## The Shepherdess

"For there is no difference between Jew and Gentile–the same Lord is Lord of all and richly blesses all who call on him, for, "Everyone who calls on the name of the Lord will be saved." As a society we must be tolerant. There are many religions and each believes in God even though the name, nomenclature, and beliefs differ. Common traits cross religions—one such example it the name of God. In the majority of religions, the name for God includes the 'AH' sound - God, Yahweh, Allah, and Buddah. Customs are similar as well. Tithing, the Eucharist, a holy book of teachings, group prayer–these common threads mark many religions. Believers have much in common, which should be a basis for acceptance of one another. In God's family we are all one.

Generally, being a Christian means believing in only one God, the God of all and creator of the universe, of all that is seen and unseen. Christianity includes belief in Jesus Christ as God in the flesh, born of a virgin, without sin–the chosen Messiah—that Jesus suffered and died on the cross for our sins, was buried and rose from the dead to ascend into heaven and will return one day. We are all sinners, guilty before God, deserving of judgment, but we will receive salvation through His holy grace. Acts 16: 31 tells us, "Believe in the Lord Jesus, and you will be saved." Eternal joy in the holy kingdom is a gift from God which we believers look forward to. Finally, there is the sense of community. Christians should attend church to encourage moral and spiritual enrichment.

These beliefs are the blueprint by which we each formulate our personal code of ethics. It sets the standard and forms the basis of our relationships and interactions with others. Each day we encounter words and incidents that mesh or conflict with this blueprint. If we were to structure a continuum with God at one end and Satan at the other, a wide range of actions and behaviors would lie between the two. To be open-minded is important, but we must be cautious as well. We must trust in our inner wisdom and guidance. These same experiences and associations help us grow as individuals and shape our value systems, provide us with a framework that lends credibility to our values. Mom has shown abundantly that God's light is the beacon in the darkness. We can set our sight on God and the path will become ever clear.

What determines our value system? Values are usually instilled in us by our parents but include significant others along the way. Our values determine how we respond to situations and deal with life. If within us lies a desire to live a faithful life honoring God, we no doubt inherited a strong ethical/moral value system and strive to be a person of integrity. We work hard each day to continue to make progress on our journey through life, treating others fairly and with respect. Teaching us this blueprint by example, Mom shows how kindness, humility and helping the poor and needy are virtues.

Yes, Mom makes it seem so easy. Her actions teach us the "inside out" model of helping others. We start with the

## The Shepherdess

family—focus at first on getting and keeping the immediate family on track—and then branch out to neighbors, community, the world. In this way all of humanity can be transformed through the strength of family. Simply, strong family units create caring communities. Caring communities create nations of integrity. Nations of integrity create a peaceful world.

Another way to make a difference is to simplify our lives. Get rid of clutter. Change the focus from things to people. Cultivate meaningful relationships. Start thinking "we" instead of "me." Minimize the ego. When we think beyond our immediate narcissism and consider the needs of others, we live the gospel. Its message comes to life. All of society benefits.

Integrated into our daily interactions, formal religious instruction furnishes the cornerstone for success. However, it's not just an intellectual understanding of these principles that sets believers apart. Christians implement these principles because they reside in their hearts. Warm, caring hearts—not the mere knowledge that something is the "right thing to do"—drives action. When the heart leads, the mind follows. Hebrews 4:7 reminds us, "Today, if you hear his voice, do not harden your hearts." The Lord asks that we let our hearts provide the basis for our daily interactions and relationships. Think of each daily relationship in this way. If we take this same message 'to heart,' would we not treat everyone with respect? We would extend to everyone, not only authority figures such as bosses, but also to people we may not even care for–those we "just don't get along with' or even outright enemies. The message is clear. We must keep our hearts open to love. We must care for everyone. This is the key to transforming our relationships and, by using Mom's "inside out" principle, the world itself.

At times, lending our hearts free rein leads us to face the "gray zones" of formal religious teaching and training. These occasions serve to gauge our own internal beliefs and prompt us to question if we are totally aligned with the beliefs and teachings of the Church. For me, one of these topics has long been the concept of limbo.

For centuries the Church has taught that, to be saved, we must be baptized. Baptism, Christians know and believe, is *the* way to salvation. But then–what of tiny, innocent babies who die before baptism, through no fault of their own? Since the thirteenth century, when it adopted this concept, the Catholic Church held that these children went into *limbus infantium*, better known as limbo, a place between heaven and hell. In 2006 Pope Benedict rejected the concept, saying, "Limbo has never been a defined truth of faith." I was pleased to hear this clarification. I have always believed it is the Church's responsibility to provide everyone with hope, especially grieving parents who lost a child, and to reinforce the message that Jesus came to die for us all. My heart has told me that our loving Father would never close the door of his kingdom to vulnerable, innocent babes who had never had the opportunity to be baptized.

## The Shepherdess

We are all on journeys to spiritual attainment in this parenthesis of time we call 'life.' Reams have been written about spirituality, spiritual principles, and pathways to enlightenment. Many of these books help us reflect on the process of our journey to spirituality and teach us the fundamental truth of how to know God. The principles and concepts themselves are known by many names—e.g., coincidence, intention, positive energy and attraction, conflict as a result of trying to control or have power over others, giving and receiving to live a life of abundance, gratitude, unconditional love or relating to others in a manner that brings out their best, inspiration or God working through us to bring out *our best* (also known as being "in-spirit"). These principles communicate attitude and awareness. My own reading of such books has only shown me how closely linked Mom is to God—notwithstanding her understanding and daily use of spiritual principles. Her belief system, thoughts, and actions seem in perfect alignment. It was no coincidence that she was born to immigrant Catholic parents; it was divine design. Once someone told me that God lets us choose our own parents to provide us lessons by which we can learn and grow. The more I thought on this concept, the more I liked the idea. In Mom's case, her own humble, hard-working immigrant folks built the foundation for her spiritual base. Early in her life this framework cultivated her spiritual awakening and led her to a strong connection with and love of the Blessed Mother.

As a result of her prayer energy, Mom's connection to God expanded. Her daily attendance at Mass sustained her. With God as her primary energy source, she has had no need to manipulate or dominate others. She has been able to minimize or rid conflict often caused by such egocentric needs. As a result, her relationships are loving and kind, with minimal conflict. She remembers and echoes Jesus' words from Matthew 25:40, "I tell you the truth, whatever you did for one of the least of these brothers of mine, you did for me." Her faith and connection has furnished her a template to answer *all* her needs, spiritual and other.

Along the way, she has cultivated two characteristic traits–positive attitude and awareness. Early in her life, she realized that her spiritual path was right before her. This path meant raising eleven wonderful children in a partnership with the Lord. In addition, she would work for the church, help the poor, tend to the sick, and be there for all of humanity. With her mission so well understood, her life's flow of "meaningful coincidences" has accelerated.

For as long as I can remember, Mom has always had the ability to love everyone unconditionally. Her seeing beauty in each face uplifts and brings out the best in others. Her own children have been huge benefactors in this regard, but they are but a fraction of those she has touched. Indeed, a "Midas touch" seems to envelope Mom. Her uncanny way of knowing life's secrets and her unconditional acceptance of God's will puts her at a far higher level of spiritual consciousness, whereby her strong belief system seems to

## The Shepherdess

form a "coat of armor" to shield and protect her from the pain that the great majority of us endure in life.

Mom's ability to reframe any situation to discern its positive side provides her with so much comfort and peace. It takes work—literally, years of practice–to hone such a skill for accentuating the positive even in the face of the worst adversities. This is a choice we can all make. Is the glass half full or half empty? With mastery comes reward and an overwhelming sense of peace and acceptance.

While Mom has always been such a positive person, she is equally realistic. It is not enough just to wish for something. We must focus on *making* things happen. Mom values hard work as a fundamental ingredient to breed success for life's challenges and pursuits. It is this *work ethic* she has demonstrated to us all.

Finally, Mom has always been extremely *grateful* for what is in her life. Moreover, declaring gratitude to God for all our daily blessings and abundance is a step to attracting more of the same into our lives. Our thoughts are powerful, and can contribute to creating and manifesting goodness and abundance. Simply consider the law of attraction. When we compound positive energy and when we believe and gratefully see the best in a situation, we can bring into our lives the fulfillment of our wishes and desires. Also true, however, is the converse. Think constantly "I wish I didn't have so much debt" and as a result you're focusing on debt. Instead, think "I'm grateful that I am able to make all my payments." Such places the emphasis on gratitude and on knowing that you have the ability to pay.

When these gifts do in fact show up, we need to be grateful again. We need to thank and praise the Lord. Yes, gratitude produces an energy which attracts more gifts. A wealth of gratitude, in turn, allows like to attract like.

Intention is, by one definition, determination to act in a certain way. Another defines intention as the purpose of a prayer, Mass, or pious act. Our intentions integrate our desires, and we prioritize our needs and desires. Praying for people and their own special intentions comes second nature to Mom, it is a well-integrated part of her life's mission. Her unselfish prayers and asking God to provide for the needs of others distinguishes her as a true advocate for the needy. In both thought and prayer she continually puts others first, far ahead of her own intentions, drawing consistently from faith, hope, and trust for the Lord to answer her prayers. Such has served to allow her to open the door, to connect directly with God to fulfill her prayers. Forever open and receptive, she knows that God will answer. As Luke 11:9 counsels, "So I say to you, Ask and it will be given to you; Seek and you will find; Knock, and the door will be opened to you." Mom knows this first hand. God always answers. It may not seem like it at the time, but on careful reflection we can see God's divine wisdom in everything that occurs.

Christianity consists of a number of denominations, each similar but distinct. As a Lutheran, I could see that the role of Mary was a significant departure from such in Catholicism. In researching this difference, Catholics

## The Shepherdess

believe that Mary is the mother of Jesus Christ, who is fully God and fully man. Therefore she is called theotokos (God-Bearer) and 'mother of God." Catholics, like Protestants, believe that Mary was a virgin when she gave birth to Jesus. However, Catholics and Orthodox Christians believe that Mary remained a Virgin her entire life. Catholics believe she was conceived without original sin in order to be a sinless bearer of God incarnate, Jesus Christ, and is known as the Immaculate Conception. Such purity resulted not through Mary's merits but through God's grace. The Orthodox, too, believe Mary was sinless when bearing Jesus, but the moment at which she became sinless is still open to debate. Catholics and Orthodox both believe that after Mary completed the course of her early life, she was assumed in heaven, similar to the way the great profit Elijah was. Mary is the mother of us and the mother of the church. Mom has always had a special relationship with the Blessed Mother. Mary has always been an intercessor and thus the focus of Mom's special prayers and intentions since she was a little girl. The Blessed Mother represents hope, faith and love to Mom.

Each year, the Feast of the Annunciation marks the anniversary of the conception of Jesus. It has been more than 2000 years since that special day. The Archangel Gabriel received Mary's response to God's request that she bear a child, the son of God. In Luke 1:38 Mary responds, "May it be done to me according to your word." This act of acceptance changed the course of history. The son of

God would now become human. Mary truly trusted the Lord and accepted His request with her whole heart. As Cardinal Newman has stated in part, "Mary passed on to Jesus his physical features. Her motherhood went beyond that as she formed his human character. Mary trained and educated Him as any mother brings up a child. Her virtues would have an impact on Him. We each realize that our mother's influence is recognizable in us and we can reasonably conclude that Mary's influence was evident in Jesus. Mary was more than merely the biological mother of the Lord Jesus. Mary's task in the Incarnation was not over with the birth of Jesus in the stable at Bethlehem. As with all mothers, the birth was only the beginning and it was followed by daily care and education. Mary continuously provided the foundation and nourishment for Jesus as he grew from infancy to childhood, into adolescence, and to young manhood. I believe that just as Mary was a wonderful mother for Jesus, she desires to be a loving mother to each of us. She raised him in a household of faith. She had the remarkable experience of forming him in both a human and spiritual sense."

With this experience, we should be very excited to ask for Mary's assistance and maternal help. Mom has continuously prayed to Mary her entire life for all her needs and those of her family, especially her eleven children. Just as one turns to their own mother for assistance, Mom prays to Mary many times using the 'Hail Mary' prayer in addition to others. The renowned Cardinal Newman stated,

## The Shepherdess

"When your heart is anxious, turn to Mary and say 'Mary, put my heart at peace.' When your mind is too busy, look to Mary and pray, 'Mary, settle down my mind.' When you want to grow and deepen your life, look to Mary and beg, 'Mary, just as you have helped Jesus to grow in wisdom and grace, help me also to advance on the spiritual path which God has laid out for me.'"

The Bible tells us that when Jesus was on the cross, he looked down and saw Mary, his mother and John, his beloved disciple. He said to his mother, "Woman, behold your son!" Then he said to the disciple, "Behold your mother!" At this point in time, Mary became the mother of all the disciples of Jesus. Pope John Paul in his 1987 encyclical *Redemptoris Mater* said, "This is not only John, who at that hour stood at the foot of the Cross together with the Mother of Jesus, but it is also true of every disciple of Christ, of every Christian."

This strong affirmation by Pope John Paul demonstrates Mary's role in the Catholic church. She is the "Mother of all Believers." This wonderful example of motherhood has been at the forefront of Mom's beliefs since her days attending Sorrowful Mother's Novena every Friday night at St. Casmir's church as a little girl, with her own mother. Looking back to my first encounter with Mom on that sunny fall afternoon in 1972 some thirty-six years ago, I remember the picture of the Mother of Perpetual Help holding baby Jesus so vividly in my mind. I couldn't put my finger on why it had such an impression on me that day and tried to comprehend its significance. As time went by, I could see that the maternal skills that Mom not only embraced, but also passed on to her children, are traits of the Blessed Mother. Mom has fostered a home filled with faith. She had helped all of her sheep not only to recognize the Lord, but also to grow with God's good grace.

A short time ago, I attended Mass on a Tuesday night. Our Mother of Perpetual Help was the theme of the homily. The priest explained that MPH was the gateway that allows us to have a wonderful relationship with Jesus. Her self-sacrifice and willingness to share her son with the world is her gift of perpetual love and help. As you gaze at the MPH picture, you notice that Mary is not looking down at her son, Jesus, but rather she is looking 'outward'. She stares 'outward' to implore us to embrace her son and to accept his love. Mom has always embraced MPH and followed in her footsteps. Her whole life she too has had an outward vision and a desire to share her very own gifts with the world. Reflecting back to the first time I viewed the picture of MPH in the Wiencek living room in 1972, I did not understand the significance. This new revelation brought a new perspective and helped me understand why the picture was so mesmerizing and seemed to draw me into the house and into this family.

# Beth Ann

*Beth was the last child born, the baby of the family, born on March 27, 1968. Beth's name was chosen by her siblings. When I coached at Our Lady of Good Hope, coaches stayed with the same team for four years and took the team from fifth through eighth grade. It was Beth's class that I coached. Beth was a cheerleader for our team. It wasn't very difficult to motivate the team with Beth and the rest of her charming friends on the cheering squad. The boys seemed to play a little harder when the girls were present to cheer them on!*

## St. Elizabeth Ann Seton

Dear God, You blessed Elizabeth Ann Seton with gifts of grace as wife and mother, educator and foundress, so that she might spend her life in service to your people. Through her example and prayers, may we learn to express our love for You. In love for our fellow man and women, we ask this through Our Lord Jesus Christ, Your Son, who lives and reigns with You and the Holy Spirit, one God, forever and ever.

As I interviewed Mom for this book on Tuesday, July 7, 2007, we sat in chairs on her front lawn beside a statue of the Blessed Mother. Two small evergreen trees, given to Mom years earlier, flanked the statue. It was a beautiful day, and the sun's brilliant light glimmered prominently on the statue of Mary. As we began with a prayer for guidance, a beautiful, yellow-brown

## The Shepherdess

butterfly made its way towards us and, during our prayer, fluttered over Mom's shoulder. For years the Wienceks had always had the uncanny luck of spotting butterflies at significant times in their lives. Members had spotted them at weddings and other special events. However, the most significant sightings occurred at the funerals of Mary, Pat, and Dad. And why not? Butterflies represent new life. A butterfly is an insect that has gone through a metamorphosis to become a magnificent, mesmerizing creature. No wonder this creature is a universal symbol for rebirth!

When a person is baptized or accepts Jesus as our Lord and Savior, he is reborn in the faith. And, as a loved one dies and enters the heavenly kingdom, a butterfly can be symbolic. Some think that such is a sign that their late loved one has passed to the other side and has "received their wings."

We discussed a number of topics. One which I really wanted to touch on was her understanding of sin. I asked Mom what she thought, and she replied, "Well, I don't really look at it as sin. I always say Jesus; you're always good to me. I never want to hurt you in any way. And if I did hurt Him in any way it would be considered 'sin.' That's how I talk to Jesus–I don't ever want to hurt you Jesus. As a result, I try to do the will of God and be good." I persisted. I asked Mom if she thought there were genuinely *bad* people. "There is something good in everyone and you need to get it to the forefront and bring it out of them," she told me. "What really helps is a person's friends. They are a huge influence on an individual." What did Mom think happens to sinners after they die? Mom replied, "They may go to purgatory if a venial sin is involved." Did she truly believe in purgatory? "Yes, I believe in purgatory very much, but that it is a temporary stage. That's why we have Masses said for our beloved and we pray for them. Because of our prayers, they may be granted heaven," she elaborated. "Purgatory is like limbo, it's a happy place, but not glorious. These people never see God. Our ultimate happiness is to be with the Lord."

The next topic regarded hell. She said, "Purgatory is nothing like hell. Hell is devastating, oh mercy, keep us all away from hell. Saints have visions of hell and tell us it's absolutely the worst. If you die in a state of mortal sin, you are going to go to hell. That is a fact. Mortal sin means in full consent of your will." I often wondered about suicides. I asked Mom what she thought happened to people who take their own lives? She responded with commitment and emphasis, "There I say we have a merciful God. He understands and forgives them. That's how I feel. We do not have a vengeful God–he creates all of us for Him."

Most Christians try to live lives modeled after that of Jesus. A few years ago a campaign started using bracelets inscribed with the letters "WWJD"–"What Would Jesus Do?" to remind everyone to live and act as our Lord did. The ultimate goal of Christians is to attain the final pass– to rejoin our loving Father in His heavenly kingdom. A friend of Mom's once said, "When Dorothy's time finally

## The Shepherdess

comes, St. Peter himself will come and personally escort her to Heaven." Definitely a compliment, yes! But then, I can't think of a more fitting escort for a woman who has dedicated her entire life to others.

John 14:20 reads, "On that day, you will know that I am in our Father, and you in me, and I in you." Our life's ambition is to attain life eternal in the heavenly kingdom. On our day of judgment we will each review our lives and perceive our accomplishments as well as failures. For our gifts and talents we will be asked to account. Did we use all that God gave us to the best of our abilities? Many believe that there is an archive, containing all that has happened since the Creation, and some say that these records of our earthly deeds determine our fates. Once I heard a priest consider philosophically questions God would or would not ask as we departed the earth and arrived before the gates of Paradise:

- God would not ask us the size of our home. He would ask, "How many people did you welcome into your home?"
- God would not ask us the model of car we drove. He would ask, "How many people did you offer to give rides to when they were in need?"
- God would not ask us our profession. He would ask, "Did you work hard to the best of your ability? Did you serve others?"
- God would not ask us what religion we were. He would ask, "Were you faithful and did you do God's

work?"
- God would not ask us the brands of clothes we wore. He would ask, "Did you share your clothes and donate them to others in need?"
- God would not ask us how tall we were. He would ask, "Did you reach out to others in need?"
- God would not ask us how many hours a week we worked. He would ask, "Did you volunteer your time and talents to assist others?"
- God would not ask us how many degrees we had. He would ask, "Were you smart enough to recognize Me?"

Life on earth is filled with many miracles. Some we readily see. Others remain hidden from our understanding. We must strive to understand these wonders that God provides. By paying attention to even the relatively minor gifts the Lord gives us, we allow our lives to be filled with more joy and appreciate our environment even more. Allowing our divine nature to come to the forefront gives us the opportunity to put others' needs first. This mindset lets us perceive God's glorious wonders. We must continue to pray that we are able to remain strong on our path to the Lord and that we are blessed with God's graces. Mom has always chosen this path. Even the least of God's wonders she relishes with gratitude and love. Last year I sent her some questions about her life. I asked her to share how her life has been influenced by the power of God's love, blessings, and good graces. She replied as follows:

## The Shepherdess

<u>On a daily basis, what is your source of strength?</u>

"My source of strength on a daily basis are my daily Masses and the Rosary. When the children were all at home, every night we said one decade of the Rosary, actually completing one Rosary a week."

<u>Who has made a difference in your spirituality?</u>

"When I was a child, each Friday my mother would take me by the hand to Sorrowful Mother's Novena each Friday. I really didn't understand it, but the Blessed Mother must have been happy to see a child come with her mother. The Capuchins at St. Elizabeth and now the priests at Our Lady of Good Hope were also instrumental in shaping my spirituality. They not only shaped me, but the whole parish community. Father Nerius and Father Stollenwerk were very instrumental early on. What dear friends I have cultivated at church. Another group I must mention is my quilting group, the 'Quilting Ladies.' The seven of us meet every other Wednesday – there is never any gossip, just fun stories.

<u>Was there ever a time when your faith was tested?</u>

"My faith was tested when I was told that I had colon cancer. Father Peter Carek gave me the Sacrament of the Sick and I was totally prepared to die. The surgery was scheduled on December 8 (on the Feast of the Immaculate Conception of the Blessed Mother). I thought that the Blessed Mother would swoop me up that day and whisk me to heaven. The Lord had other plans. As the kids bought their new homes, I did all the sewing treatments for the windows, beds, etc. When that became too much, I resorted to making quilts for family, friends and the needy.

How has God's power shaped you?

"God's enormous power has helped me to survive all the trials and tribulations of raising a large family. He provided for our material needs and always provided me with emotional support when I needed it most. That was so important. As the years went by, the grandchildren became a huge blessing and joy–the perfect set up, love them and leave them."

Did you ever encounter a situation where you felt you couldn't go on?

"There were many a day that I would have liked to give up or surrender, but through the grace of God I persevered in my prayer life and marriage.

How have God's blessings affected your life?

"God's blessings have helped our commitment in our marriage for 55 years. Our faith and trust in the Lord were our testimony to God. Erv and I were truly blessed with eleven children. Another great blessing was finding our home on 38th street. Mother of Perpetual Help heard my plea for a home that was inexpensive and accommodating for a large family. After living here for 40 years, I so enjoy my lovely home."

How have you been God's light in the world?

"My daily visits to the Eucharistic Chapel and daily Mass are enough of an example, without preaching, to influence our children in spirituality. Erv and I dedicated

## The Shepherdess

our family to the Sacred Heart of Jesus. When we were at St. Elizabeth, I went on a three-day retreat out of town each year. Erv encouraged me to go and he stayed home with the kids. What a guy! When I came home, I was refreshed and rejuvenated for another year. Now in retirement, when I receive many religious prayer leaflets and rosaries, I give them to the grandchildren – hoping their spirituality will grow as the years go by. In closing, please pray for me as I always remember to pray for you. Thanks be to God."

On May 3, 2008, Patricia's oldest son, Andrew, was married. Andy had his MBA from Cardinal Stritch and was working in finance; Deanna was a registered nurse working at a local hospital. The wedding, very beautiful, was at St. Sebastian's Church, on Milwaukee's north side. It was difficult for the family to experience the joy the couple shared without Pat sharing the occasion. A beautiful bouquet of yellow roses (Pat's favorite color) stood near the altar to symbolize Pat's presence. Mom served as the "Lay Distributor" for Communion, which brought back wonderful memories for everyone. Once again Mom was strong, and her guidance made for a magnificent day for everyone. The reception was held at Botanical Gardens Whitnall Conservatory. The dinner was excellent and the family celebrated and danced until late in the night. Especially fitting was when the band played "We are Family" by Sister Sledge. Everyone danced. It was truly a time of unity, as the song expresses.

Last year, Mom sent a picture to each of the families.

The picture offers a verse written over a background of white roses. The verse reads "Be generous with your love. Be generous with your prayer time. Be generous with the poor and needy." Below is a heart-shaped fiftieth-anniversary picture of Mom and Dad. "This picture tells the whole story," Mom said. "It's our legacy. Pray a lot, help the needy, and keep a strong faith in God."

As a young girl, Mom's favorite flower was always the daffodil. Since Mom is an Aries (her birthday falls on March 30), this spring flower holds a special sentimental value in this regard. The daffodil is a symbol of rebirth, of the new beginnings that springtime brings. In England the flower is referred to as the "Lent Lilly" because it blooms around Lent. This has always been an important time for the Wiencek family. Not only is Lent a time of prayer, reconciliation, and preparation for Easter, it is a time to reflect on the importance of family and to remember Mary Beth and her quest to reveal the true meaning of Easter. Mom readily admits that her favorite flower today is the calla lily, followed by roses, reminiscent of St. Therese.

When I think of flowers, my thoughts turn to open meadows, pastures, grazing sheep, the beauty of nature, and the glory of God. Jesus, ruler of the universe, is our King, but He chose to rule like a shepherd. By this I mean that He came to serve and included everyone at his table. Yes, the Lord's table *is* the place where saints and sinners meet as friends, a place where saints realize they are forgiven sinners, a place where sinners can become saints

## The Shepherdess

through His holy grace. Mathew 25: 31-33 describes as follows, "When the Son of Man comes in his glory, and all the angels with him, He will sit on his throne in heavenly glory. All the nations will be gathered before Him, and He will separate the people one from another as the shepherd separates the sheep from the goats. He will put the sheep on the right, and the goats on the left."

We all seek to be viewed as the sheep, not the goats, as those destined to be saved for eternity. Jesus, our loving shepherd, does not choose to exert control over his flock. Rather, he gently gathers us, and wishes to include everyone in the joy of everlasting life. The word "my" seems to be missing from Jesus' vocabulary. His invitation extends to all. Maybe if more of us left the "me" out of our vocabularies, the world would be a better place. The following story illustrates well the distinction between "my" and "our":

A Catholic pastor lived in the church rectory. His extremely hard-working housekeeper came in every day to cook and clean. Repeatedly she would make remarks like "Father, I cleaned 'your' coffee pot," and he would correct her by saying, "No, Sarah, it is 'our' coffee pot." The next day she told Father "I watered 'your' plant." Again he corrected her, with "No, Sarah, it is 'our' plant." That night the bishop came over for dinner. While the bishop and the pastor dined, Sarah went upstairs to tidy up Father's room. Suddenly several screams erupted. The bishop and the pastor ran to the bottom of the stairs, to meet an ashen-faced

Sarah scurrying down. "Sarah, what happened?" asked the pastor. "Is everything all right?" Sarah replied, "No Father! A mouse just ran under '*our*' bed!"

Helping the unfortunate and not judging the "goats" all around us is not easy. Years ago, Christine brought home a request from high school. A nun was seeking anyone willing to write a young man incarcerated at Waupun Correctional Center. Mom decided to accept, and wrote him a letter. They corresponded several times a month for over a year. He looked forward to her letters of hope. Suddenly he stopped writing. Two months later Mom received her last letter and an explanation. He had escaped and had thought seriously of coming to see her. He really wanted to come, he said, but realized that it would not be fair to her. He had learned an important lesson; to put another's needs ahead of his own.

Mom has been an inspirational shepherd and matriarch. But, like any leader, she looks to the future; she knows she will not live forever. When her time does come, no doubt she will click her heels together like another famous Dorothy and remark, "There's no place like home." Yes, she has an eagerly awaited reservation to return, become one with the Lord, and reunite with the members of her family. Recently she chose Terry to assume her matriarch role. Hearing of it, Nicole jokingly coined Terry as the "Matriarch in Training," or M.I.T. Terry said that she will need years of training. As I thought years ago, if Terry turns out to be even half of her mother, I will consider myself

## The Shepherdess

blessed beyond measure. No, the apple did not fall far from the tree. I am blessed.

Not too long ago Mom found it difficult to make her quilts. Most are large and cumbersome, and the toil started to take a toll. One day Margaret's husband Dean suggested to Mom that she do smaller, less demanding tasks. He fondly remembered her bibs for all the grandbabies—bibs so soft and unique but functional. Might the bibs provide an outlet? Over the years many had remarked about their beauty and usefulness. After some thought, Mom left her quilting days behind. Quilts, move over! Make way for bibs! Within a short time her bibs, too, were unique yet shared gifts of love. By now she has made too many to count, and is still excited to use her God-given talents to help others.

Recently Mom learned that I was writing this book about her. She was embarrassed, surprised, quite taken back by this tribute to her life. As always, she started thinking of what she might do to help. For one thing, she felt that the task required compensation—and mailed me a check for $300. In disbelief, I responded by telling her that I relish writing about topics that inspire me. I felt honored, I told her, to work on such a project about someone who is such a legitimate model of God's good grace. Mom replied with a near-apology. Originally she wanted to send me $500, she confided, but had to send $100 to each of two charities for the poor. Even as I type these words, I think of this woman of limited income and I am amazed.

A few months ago I asked Mom's best friend, Theresa Bergs, if she could mention one trait that sets Mom apart. First, Mrs. Bergs, another earth angel, thanked us for our concern and daily phone calls to Mom. Mom was now living alone, she knew, and she appreciated the calls to check on her best friend. Next, Mrs. Bergs told me that, as Mom's *adopted sister*, she spends a great deal of time with her. As close neighbors and fellow-parishioners over the years, the two women have shared much. Before Dorothy had her driver's license, the pair would shop together weekly for their families–quite a job. Then, she told me the one thing that sets Dorothy apart is her *charisma*. "Dorothy," she said, "draws people to her. Most times when I had relatives visiting me, they didn't consider it a true visit unless they got to see Dorothy."

In February of 2008 I spoke with Father Charlie Zabler, Mom's current pastor at Our Lady of Good Hope Church. Happy to write about Mom and her relationship with the Lord, he penned the following:

*Dorothy.....*

*Every family needs a Dorothy. Every family needs a source of nurture. Every family needs someone to make the quilt and wrap us in it as a sign of the love and acceptance that surrounds us. Dorothy as wife and mother, and grandmother has seen the family grow and develop. She has guided them all wondering why her husband and children are her inspiration. If they are an inspiration to you Dorothy, it is because you nurtured those qualities in*

## The Shepherdess

*them.*

*Every faith community needs a Dorothy. Every church and assembly of God's people needs a Dorothy. Every Pastor and Minister, every saint and sinner needs a Dorothy. Who ministers to the ministers, but those who pray for them? Who ministers to saints and sinners, but those who love them? Dorothy is so precious in that her piety and devotion flows from her heart, that she might reach out to many. What would we be without Dorothy's wisdom, laughter, prayers and presence?*

*Dorothy, thank you for your witness of love in your family, neighborhood and the church.*

*Please know how much you are loved and appreciated. Your prayers and generosity, kindness, tears and laughter are indeed a sign of God's presence among us.*

Fr. Charlie Zabler

The average parishioner sees priests come and go, leave their parishes due to the needs of the diocese. Mom has seen her share. One of her favorites, Father Don Hying, was the pastor at OLGH for six-and-a-half years. Father Hying left to become a rector at St Francis Seminary, where young men study to become priests—a passion of both Mom and Patricia. Father Hying offered the following insight into his relationship with Mom:

*Dorothy Wiencek is truly an inspiration and example for all of us. Many things about her personality and life stand out for me. The first is her deep spirituality. Dorothy goes to Mass every day, spends many hours in Eucharistic adoration, prays the rosary and is completely devoted to her faith. Her relationship with Christ and the saints is a living one, filled with love and peace. I am convinced that it is her deep faith that allows Dorothy to embrace the many crosses in her life with equanimity and joy.*

*Dorothy's generosity is another outstanding attribute. From her quilting to her cooking, to visiting the sick, to raising all those children, her life has always been about others, never herself. She has truly poured herself out in Christ-like fashion for the sake of others. So many lives have been touched by her goodness, faith, love and joy, more than anyone could imagine.*

*Dorothy is one of those quiet heroes who goes about the ordinary tasks of life with a passion and conviction that makes a difference. Her smile can light up a room. Her faith can lift a weary heart. Her love is palpable. Dorothy knows who she is and where she is going. That conviction gives all of us strength we need.*

Additionally, Father Hying supplied the following words by Myles Connolly, that he felt similarly sums up Dorothy's life and contributions.

"Everybody must at one time or another have known persons...who have changed the quality of the day. They came into a room in a dark hour–a sick room, say, or a death room, a room without hope, or merely in an hour when we are lonely or discouraged. They may say little, if anything. But the shining quality of goodness radiates from them, from their mere presence, and where there was dark there is light, or the beginning of light; where there was cowardice there is courage; where there was listlessness there is love of life. Such people are the greatest of artists. For they practice the highest of the arts–the art of life itself."

As I reluctantly conclude this book, I can't help but reconsider the theme that truly inspired me to write this story of fifty-three years. We are all on life quests to understand, to know, to honor God. Along the way we celebrate the joys, and endure great pain. How much easier it is to accept the Lord in the good times than in the bad. In times of grief, many turn their backs to God. Why, we wonder, could God allow such tragedies to happen? Our human tendency is to lose faith and abandon Him. However, it is during these telling times when we are left alone that our faith is not only tested but fortified. With her resiliency despite the circumstances, Mom has taught us all the power of forgiveness and love. Her deeds have defined a path by which all of us here on earth can travel. She strongly believes what we must come to realize that God Himself has gone through grief as well. His own son suffered terribly before he was raised from the dead. God the Father truly has first-hand experience. With all the joys, pains, happiness, and sadness that Mom has experienced, never once has she budged from her belief in the Lord. With great strength and a calm demeanor, she has each time risen above the human situation to a level of enormous spiritual peace–an example to all. Never a judge of others, she has been a sponsor of faith and a model of God's good grace.

## Birk

As she herself best put it, "God's ways are not our ways. If we truly love Jesus, we will simply accept that 'God's Will' is done."

# Epilogue

# Dorothy

## "We Remember, We Celebrate, We Believe!"

In any successful organization, leadership starts at the top. A matriarch earns respect, admiration, and trust through her outstanding life skills. By all appearances, Mom is plain and simple–your average mom. She never brings attention to herself. Nonetheless, this humble demeanor has not compromised her ability to affect so many people. Her lifetime of achievement in serving is a tribute to those she has so willingly served. You could say she is the conductor on our family "faith train." Her shepherdess skills are a direct result of her faith in the Lord and desire to protect and lead others down the righteous and glorious path to eternal life. Mathew 5:48 tells us, "But you are to be perfect, even as your father in heaven is perfect."

I am most fortunate to have been blessed with two wonderful mothers in my lifetime. Each instilled a set of values and wrapped them in a cloak of love. Dorothy has used her special connection to the Blessed Mother as a foundation on which to enlighten others in their quest for salvation. Just as the Blessed Mother broadened her horizons to become the 'Mother of All Believers,' Mom has followed closely in her footsteps emulating the Blessed Mother's grace and beliefs. Mom believes in the Lord and that the truth is in God. The truth shall set you free. Based on this certainty, we can all achieve greatness in our lives simply by doing the will of God.

Directed by God to lead his people out of Egypt, Moses knew he himself would never reach the Promised Land. Even as he faced the probability of death, he put other's needs first. Mom's unselfish acts of kindness and compassion have always put others first as well.

As you forge your way down the road of life, pay close attention and look for your spiritual change agents. They will enlarge your territory. Be open, be strong, and persevere. Maintain a positive *attitude* and have a keen *awareness* of your opportunities. It's never too late to climb on board the faith train–the next one leaves on Tuesday.

We love you, Mom!

# A Generational Testament of 31 Grandchildren

What is the most important thing you have learned from Grandma?

Nicole Marie: Be generous with your love, prayer time, and with the poor and needy.

Andrew Joseph: The importance of loving one another.

Jonathan Adam: Love the Lord with all your heart.

Brian Christopher: I've learned the passion it takes to be the most diehard Brewers fan in Wisconsin!

Katherine Ann: To rejoice and celebrate the lives of the loved ones we have lost.

David Michael Patrick: With hard work, prayer, and patience, anything you set your mind to is possible.

Christopher Joseph: You have to live life to the fullest, no matter what comes in the way.

Sarah Kathryn: Profound faith in God and spiritual consciousness is imperative during the best and worst times.

Lindsay Marie: When I was about nine years old, I was at home working on homework. Grandma came over to our house and told me, "All work and no play makes Jack a dull boy."

Megan Elizabeth: The importance of giving to others out of the goodness of your heart.

Steven James: Grandma taught me to pray that the Lord provides for the needs of others.

Lauren Elizabeth: Grandma taught me that I'm Little Mary.

Ashley Christine: It doesn't matter who you pray to, because, regardless, the "Holy Spirit will guide you."

Jennifer Katherine: Grandma would always tell me "Everything good happens on a Tuesday." So every time I date my papers on Tuesdays for school, I think about Grandma always telling me this little fact of hers.

Thomas William: Enjoy the simple pleasure of good company: Watching the Packers, the Brewers, and talking with Grandma after cutting the lawn.

Matthew James: Grandma has taught me to "Never give up on your dreams."

Benjamin Dean: Grandma has shown me how to trust in God always and how to live my faith.

Timothy Jacob: Generosity can make someone's day, and look to the Lord for answers to your problems.

Dana Catherine: Grandma taught me that forgiveness is a sign of strength.

Elizabeth Ann: Grandma has taught me to never give up and to always persevere.

Peter John: Grandma has taught me to love others as they have loved you.

Kristyn Danielle: Always love and stay true to your God.

Ryan Joseph: Grandma has taught me that 'Jesus' way is the right way.

Abigail Katherine: Grandma has taught me how to give by leading by example.

Courtney Nicole: Be kind to others and pray daily.

Tricia Elizabeth: Grandma has taught me that I should always be nice to everyone I meet and pray everyday.

Elliana Catherine: Grandma has taught me that life is precious.

Margaret Elizabeth: Grandma reminds me of St. Lucy because she gives things to people. She tells me it is better to give than receive.

Charles Anthony: Grandma has taught me to pray every day.

<u>Chloe Gabrielle</u>: Grandma has taught me to love my mom and dad.

<u>Adam Christopher</u>: You can never have too many grandchildren!

# References

"The Church Letters." *Clatsop County Historical Society.* Spring, 1982.

"Conclusion on limbo known before work began." *National Catholic Reporter.* Nov 8, 2008.<findarticles.com>.

*The Family Keepsake Bible.* New International Edition. Grand Rapids, Mi.: Zonderran, 1995.

*Fatima: Through the Eyes of a Child.* Buffalo, N.Y.: Immaculate Heart Publications, 2005.

Feister, John. "Picturing Mary: A Mother's Love." *St. Anthony Messenger Magazine.* May, 2007. www.americancatholic.org.

"Franciscan Morning Prayer." *Common Prayers.* Jan 5, 2009. <uga.edu>.

Grossman, Cathy Lynn. "Many find God outside of church." *Arizona Republic* (*USA Today*). Jan 9, 2006.

—. "Most believe in angels." *USA Today.* Sept. 18, 2008.

"Guardian Angels—Celestial Servants." Softkenya.com. Mar 20, 2009. <softkenya.com>.

*The Holy Bible.* New King James Edition. Nashville: Thomas Nelson, 1994.

Kissinger, Meg. "A mother leaves a gift." *Milwaukee Journal Sentinel.* May 10 1998.

"Limbo: Pope abolishes first circle of Hell." Oct 6, 2006. <galloway.wordpress.com>.

McBride, Alfred. "The Maternity of Mary." In *The Maternity of Virgin Mary*. Nov 2, 2008. www.americancatholic.org.

McCloskey, Pat. "The Many Faces of Mary in Nazareth." *St. Anthony Messenger Magazine*. Mar, 2000. www.americancatholic.org.

"The Memorare—A Prayer for help from our Blessed Mother." Jan 3, 2009. www.catholicprayers.com.

Nolan, Kate. "Faith, cancer link studied." *Arizona Republic*. Aug 4, 2007.

—. "Nurse thinks combining faith, healing a good prescription." *Arizona Republic*. Aug 4, 2007.

Pope John Paul II. *Redemptoris Mater*. Papal Encyclical, 1987.

"Prayer for the Feast of Saint Margaret Mary Alacoque." Aug 9, 2008. <catholicdoors,com>.

"A Prayer of Healing through Worship." Jan 3, 2009. <alighthouse.com>.

"Prayer to Saint Elizabeth Ann Seaton." Aug 9, 2008. <catholicdoors.com>.

"Prayer to Saint Therese." Dec 28, 2008. <frjess.blogspot.com>.

"Prayer to St. Gerard." Catholic Supply of St. Louis, bic. Aug 9, 2008. <catholicsupply.com>.

"Prayers of St. Clare of Assisi." Jan 1, 2009. <heartsnetwork.org>.

"The Renewal Of The Consecration Of The Family To The Sacred Heart of Jesus." Jan 4, 2009. <catholicdoors,com>.

"Respirit—Unfailing-Prayer-to-St-Anthony." Jan 3, 2009. <respirit.com>.

"St. Catherine of Siena Online Memorial Tribute." Jan 3, 2009. <catholic.memorials.com>.

"St. Christina the Astonishing." Jan 3, 2009. <catholicexchange.com>.

Stohs, Nancy J. "Wedding bells ring; Mom sews." *Milwaukee Journal* (Life/Style). Jan 10, 1982.

www.ingramcontent.com/pod-product-compliance
Lightning Source LLC
Chambersburg PA
CBHW061308110426
42742CB00012BA/2098